KNOCK 'EM DEAD

with Great Answers to
Tough Interview Questions

Also by Martin John Yate . . .

Resumes That Knock 'em Dead ($7.95)

Hiring the Best ($9.95)

To order these books, or additional copies of this book, just call . . .

1-800-USA-JOBS
(In Mass., 617/268-9570)

KNOCK 'EM DEAD

with Great Answers to Tough Interview Questions

Martin John Yate

BOB ADAMS ● *BOSTON*

Acknowledgments

My thanks to the following people who in different ways have helped this book become what it is today—the only internationally published job-hunting guide of its kind.

From the employment services world: Dunhill Personnel System presidents— Brad Brin of Milwaukee, Warren Mahan of Maine, Leo Salzman of Columbus, Dave Bontempo of Southhampton, Paul and Pat Erickson of Shawnee Mission, Jim Fowler of Huntsville (and Ray Johnson), Stan Hart of Troy, Mike Badgett of Cherry Hills Village, and John Webb and everyone in beautiful San Antonio.

Thanks also to Don Kipper of Ernst & Whinney, Dan O'Brien of Grumman Aerospace, Amy Marglis and Kathy Seich of Merrill Lynch, Roger Villanueva of I.M.S., Victor Lindquist of Northwestern University, Ed Fitzpatrick of the University of Michigan, and Mary Giannini of Columbia University.

He who must be obeyed, my editor, Eric Blume, gets thanks, as do that man of vision and my publisher, Bob Adams, and the people who got this hot little book into your hands—the tireless sales representatives of Bob Adams, Inc. And special thanks to Jill, for being the brightest star in my firmament.

Published by
Bob Adams, Inc.
840 Summer Street
Boston, Massachusetts 02127

ISBN: 1-55850-953-4
ISBN: 1-55850-954-2 (paperback)

Manufactured in the United States of America
1 2 3 4 5 6 7 8 9 10
   3 4 5 6 7 8 9 10 (paperback)

Contents

you must have 4 goals: Get attention, generate interest, create a desire to know more about you, and make the company representative take action. Here are 3 easy steps that will get you closer to landing the interview.   **39**

Dedication

To your successful job hunt.

Introduction

Why another book about interviewing? Because the others stop at that critical point when the tough questions start flying. They lack the practical advice of what to do in the heat of battle. *Knock 'em Dead* will first help you to arrange the interview and then will get right to the heart of your greatest interview dread: "How on earth do I answer *that* one?" It takes command where others admit defeat.

Here, you will get over 100 of the tough, sneaky, mean and low-down questions that interviewers love to throw at you. I will show you what the interviewer wants to find out about you with each one, and explain how best to reply. After each explanation, you get a sample answer and suggestions on how to customize the sample to your individual circumstances. The examples themselves come from real life, things people like you have done on the job that got them noticed and helped them get ahead in their careers.

Perhaps you are trying to land your first job, or are returning to the workplace. Maybe you are a seasoned executive taking another step up the ladder of success. Whoever you are, this book will help you, because it shows you the basics of interviewing. You will learn that every interviewer tries to evaluate each candidate by the same three criteria: Is the candidate *able* to do the job? *willing* to put in the effort to make the job a success? and last but not least, *manageable?*

9

□ □ □

The job interview is a measured and ritualistic mating dance in which the best partners whirl away with the glittering prizes. The steps of this dance are the give-and-take, question-and-response that make meaningful business conversation. Learn the steps and you, too, can dance the dance.

Your partner in the dance, obviously, is the interviewer, who will lead with tough questions that carry subtleties hidden from the untrained ear. You will learn how to recognize these questions within questions. And with this knowledge, you will be cool, calm, and collected, while other candidates are falling apart with attacks of interview nerves.

How do you discover hidden meanings in questions? I recently heard a story about a young woman who was doing very well on an interview for a high-pressure job in a television studio. The interviewer wanted to know how she would react in the sudden, stressful situations common in T.V., and got his answer when he said, "You know, I don't really think you're suitable for the job. Wouldn't you be better off in another company?" With wounded pride, the job-hunter stormed out in a huff. She never knew how close she was, how easy it would have been to land the job. The interviewer smiled: He had caught her with a tough question. Did the interviewer mean what he said? what was *really* behind the question? how could she have handled it and landed the job? The great answers are waiting for you.

The job interview has many similarities to good social conversation. Job offers always go to the interviewee who can turn a one-sided examination of skills into a dynamic exchange between two professionals. In *Knock 'em Dead* you will learn the techniques for exciting and holding your interviewer's attention, and at the same time, for promoting yourself as the best candidate for the job.

This book will carry you successfully through the worst interviews you could ever face. It is written in four interconnected parts. "The Well Stocked Briefcase" gets you ready for the fray. You will quickly learn to build a resume with broad appeal and to use a unique customizing technique guaranteed to make your application stand out as something special. You will also learn how to tap into thousands of job openings at all levels that never reach the newspapers.

Once you are ready for action, "Getting to Square One" examines all the approaches to getting job interviews and teaches you the simple and effective ways to set up multiple interviews. This section ends with techniques to steer you successfully through those increasingly common telephone interviews.

"Great Answers to Tough Interview Questions" gives you just that, and teaches you some valuable business lessons that will contribute to your future success. All successful companies look for the same things in their employees, and everything they're looking for you either have or can develop. Not possible? I will show you the twenty key personality traits that can convey your potential for success to any interviewer.

"Finishing Touches" assures that "out-of-sight-out-of-mind" will not apply to you after you leave the interviewer's office. You will even discover how to get a job offer after you have been turned down for the position. Most important, the sum of these techniques will give you tremendous self-confidence when you go to an interview: No more jitters, no more sweaty palms.

If you want to know how business works and what savvy businesspeople look for in an employee, if you want to discover how to land the interview and then conquer the interviewer, this book is for you. *Knock 'em Dead* delivers what you need to win the job of your dreams. Now get to it, step ahead in your career, and knock 'em dead.

Martin John Yate
Sea Cliff, New York

I

The Well-Stocked Briefcase

Have you heard the one about the poor man who wanted to become a famous bear slayer? Once upon a time, in a town plagued by bears, lived a man. The man had always wanted to travel but had neither the right job nor the money. If he could kill a bear, then he could travel to other places plagued with bears and make his living as a famous bear slayer. Every day he sat on the porch and waited for a bear to come by. After many weeks of waiting, he thought he might go looking for bears. He didn't know much about them, except that they were out there.

Full of hope, he rose before dawn, loaded his single-shot musket, and headed for the forest. On reaching the edge of the forest, he raised the musket and fired into the dense undergrowth.

Do you think he hit a bear, or anything else, for that matter? Why was he bear-hunting with a single-shot musket, and why did he shoot before seeing a bear? What was his problem? Our hero couldn't tell dreams from reality. He went hunting unprepared and earned what he deserved. The moral of the tale is: when you look for a job, keep a grip on reality, go loaded for bear, and don't go off half-cocked.

Out there in the concrete "forest" of your profession hide many companies. Some major corporations, some small family affairs, and some in between. They all have something in common, and that's *problems.* To solve those problems, companies need people. Anyone who ever gets hired for any job is a problem-solver. Think about your present job function: What problems would occur if you weren't there? That's why you were hired, to take care of those problems.

Being a problem-solver is good, but companies prefer to hire someone who also understands what business is all about. There are three lessons you should remember:

> *Lesson One:* Companies are in business to make money. People have loyalty to companies; companies have loyalty only to the bottom line. They make money by being more economical and saving money. They make money by being efficient and saving time. And if they save time, they save money, and have more time to make more money.

> *Lesson Two:* Companies and you are exactly alike. You both want to make as much money as possible in as short a time as possible. This allows you to do the things you really want with the rest of your time.

> *Lesson Three:* When the economy is good, you have the whip hand and can dictate the terms. This is called a *seller's market.* When the economy is bad, the employer has the whip hand and can dictate the terms; this is called a *buyer's market.*

Lesson One tells you the three things every company is interested in. Lesson Two says to recognize that you really have the same goals as the company. Lesson Three says that anyone with any sense wants to be in a seller's market.

If you look for jobs one at a time, you put yourself in a buyer's market. If you implement my advice in *Knock 'em Dead,* you will have multiple interviews because you'll be able to handle the toughest questions, and you'll get multiple job offers. This will give you the whip hand and will put you in a seller's market.

Operating in a seller's market requires knowing who, where, and what your buyers are in the market for, then being ready with the properly packaged product.

In this section, you will see how to identify all the companies that could be in need of your services. You will discover names of the president, those on the board, those in management; company sales volume; complete lines of company services or products; and size of the outfit. You will evaluate and package your professional skills in a method guaranteed to have appeal to every employer. And you will discover highly desirable professional skills you never thought you had.

A well-stocked briefcase requires more than looking idly through the want ads. It means a little discipline, a little effort. But aren't your professional goals worth the effort? It will take a couple of days' work to get you loaded for bear.

Your first action should be a trip to the library (taking sufficient paper and pens). On the way, purchase push-pins, a large-scale area map, and some stick-on labels—and rustle up a three-foot piece of string. Take some sandwiches; there is no feeling in the world like eating lunch on the library steps.

1.
Discovering What's Out There

At the library, walk in purposefully and ask for the reference section. When you find it, wander around for a few minutes before staking a claim. You will discover that libraries are a good place to watch the human race, so get the best seat in the house. Make sure you have a clear view of the librarian's desk. When you need a rest, that's where all the comic relief takes place.

There are a number of reference books you can consult, and they are listed in the Bibliography. I won't waste space teaching you how to use them here—the librarian will be happy to do that.

Your goal is to identify and build personalized dossiers on the companies in your chosen geographic area. Do not be judgmental about what and who they might appear to be: you are fishing for possible job openings, so cast your net wide and list them all.

Take a pad of paper, and using a separate sheet for each company, copy all the relevant company information onto that piece of paper. So that we agree on "relevant," take a look at the example on the following page.

Here, you see the names of the company's president and chairman of

<u>Corporation, Inc.</u>

Headquarters:
123 Main Street
Boston MA 02127

Main phone: 617/555-1200
Personnel (Joseph Smith, Director): 617/555-1234

President: Richard Johnson (for 3 yrs.)
COB: William Jones (for 2 yrs.)

Director of Word Processing Services: Peter Lee

Company produces a complete line of office machines: calculators, adding machines, typewriters (electric, electronic, manual), telephones, computerized switching systems, and a wide range of peripheral equipment. Employs 1300, all in Massachusetts.

This location is primarily an administrative facility, but it provides all services for the firm (research, repairs, operations, word processing). Manufacturing facilities located in Worcester (calculators, telephone equipment, peripherals) and Wakefield (typewriters, computers).

Sales (1985): $334.3 million
Profits: +5% from 1984

Recently acquired Disko, Inc. (Braintree, MA), a software firm (looks like it's diversifying ???). Maybe has something big in the works (possible merger with The Bigg Corporation)

the board, a description of the complete lines of company services and/or products, the size of the company, and the locations of its various branches. Of course, if you find other interesting information, copy it down, by all means. For instance, you might come across information on growth or shrinkage in a particular area of a company; or you might read about recent acquisitions the company has made. Write it down.

All this information will help you shine at the interview in three different ways. Your knowledge creates a favorable impression when first meeting the company; that you made an effort is noticed. That no one else bothers is a second benefit. And third, the combination says that you respect the company, and therefore, by inference, the interviewer; this helps set you apart from the herd.

All your effort has an obvious short-term value in helping you win job offers. It also has value in the long term, because you are building a personalized reference work of your industry/specialty/profession that will help you throughout your career whenever you wish to make a job change.

Unfortunately, no single reference work is complete. Their very size and scope means that most are just a little out of date at publication time. Also, no single reference work lists every company. Because you don't know what company has the very best job for you, you need to research as many businesses in your area as possible, and therefore you will have to look through additional reference books.

Be sure to check out any specialized guides mentioned in the Bibliography, including the *Standard & Poor's Register* and your state manufacturing directory.

At the end of the day, pack up and head home for some well-deserved troughing and sluicing. Remember to purchase a map of your area, push-pins, and small size stick-on labels for implementing the next step of your plan.

Put your map on the wall. Attach the string to a push-pin, stick the pin on the spot where you live, and draw concentric circles at intervals of one mile. In a short space of time, you will have defaced a perfectly good map, but you'll have a *physical* outline of your job-hunting efforts.

Next, take out the company biographies prepared at the library and write "#1" on the first. Find the firm's location on the map and mark it with a push-pin. Finally, mark an adhesive label "#1" and attach it to the head of the pin. As you progress, a dramatic picture of your day's work appears. Each pin-filled circle is a territory that needs to be covered, and each of those pins represents a potential job.

It is likely you will be back at the library again, finishing off this reference work and preparing your resume. The research might take a few days. Try walking to the library the next time. Not only is it cheaper (a sound reason in itself), but the exercise is very important to you. You are engaged in a battle of wits, and the healthier you are physically, the sharper you will be mentally. You need your wits about you, because there are always well-qualified people looking for the best jobs. Yet it is not the most qualified who always get the job. It is the person who is best prepared that wins every time. Job hunters who knock 'em dead at the interview are those who do the homework and preparation that a failure will not do. Do a little more walking. Do a little more research.

□ □ □

Almost everybody looking for a new job buys the newspaper and then carefully misuses it. A recent story tells of a job hunter who started by waiting for the Sunday paper to be published. He read the paper and circled six jobs. Called the first to find it had already been filled, and in the process, got snubbed by someone whose voice had yet to break, requesting that he write in the future and send a resume. As anything is better than facing telephone conversations like that, the job hunter didn't call the other five companies, but took a week to write a resume that no one would read, let alone understand. Sent it to a dozen companies. Waited a week for someone to call. Waited another week. Kicked the cat. Felt bad about that, worse about himself, and had a couple of drinks. Phone rang, someone was interested in the resume but, unfortunately, not in someone who slurred his words at lunchtime. Felt worse, stayed in bed late. Phone rings: an interview! Felt good, went to the interview. They will contact in a few days. They don't, and in the calls to them, everybody is mysteriously unavailable. The job hunter begins to feel like a blot on God's landscape. . . . This is obviously an extreme example, but the story is a little too close to the bone for many, and it illustrates the wrong way to use the paper when you're looking for a job.

Unfortunately, folks usually use either the newspaper *or* reference books, but rarely both. They run the risk of ending up in the buyer's market. Not a good place to be.

While reference books give you bags of hard information about a company, they tell you little about specific job openings. Newspapers, on the other hand, tell you about specific jobs that need filling now, but give you few hard facts about the company. The two types of research should complement each other. Often you will find ads in the newspaper for companies you have already researched. What a powerful combination of information this gives you going in the door to the interview!

The correct utilization of newspapers is to identify all companies that are currently hiring. Write down the pertinent details of each particular job opening on a separate piece of paper, as you did earlier with the reference books. Include the company's name, address, phone number, and contact names.

In addition to finding openings that bear your particular title, look for all the companies that regularly hire for your field. The fact that your job is not being advertised does not mean a company is not looking for you; if a company is in a hiring mode, a position for you might be available. In the instances when a company is active but has not been advertising specifically for your skills, write down all relevant company contact data. It should be contacted; you could be the solution to a problem that has only just arisen.

It is always a good idea to examine back issues of the newspaper. These can provide a rich source of job opportunities that remain unfilled from prior advertising efforts.

The reason you *must* use a combination of reference books and advertisements is that companies tend to hire in cycles. When you rely exclusively on newspapers, you miss those companies just about to start or just ending their hiring cycles. This comprehensive research is the way to tap what the business press refers to as the "hidden" job market. It is paramount that you have as broad a base as possible—people know people who have *your* special job to fill.

With the addition of all these companies to your map, you will have a glittering panorama of prospects, the beginnings of a dossier on each one, and an efficient way of finding any company's exact location. This is useful for finding your way to an interview and in evaluating the job offers coming your way.

Adequate research and preparation is the very foundation for performing well at interviews. And the more interviews you have, the more your research skills will increase; they are the first step to putting yourself in a seller's market.

2.
All Things to
All People

Interviewers today are continually asking for detailed examples of your past performance. They safely assume you will do at least as well (or as poorly) on the new job as you did on the old one, and so the examples you give will seal your fate. Therefore, you need to examine your past performance in a practical manner that will assure you handle these questions correctly.

This chapter will show you how to identify the examples from your past that will impress any interviewer. There is a special bonus: you will also get the correctly packaged information for an excellent resume. Two birds with one stone.

Resumes, of course, are important, and there are two facts you must know about them. First, you are going to need one. Second, no one will want to read it The average interviewer has never been trained to interview effectively, probably finds the interview as uncomfortable as you do, and will do everything possible to avoid discomfort. Resumes are therefore used more to screen people *out* than screen them *in*. So your resume must be all things to all people.

Another hurdle to leap is avoiding the specialization of your skills in the resume. A cold hard fact is that the first person to see your resume is often in the personnel department. This office screens for many different jobs and cannot be expected to have an in-depth knowledge of every specialty within the company—or its jargon.

For these reasons, your resume must be easy to read and understand, short, use words that are familiar to the reader and that have universal appeal. Most important, it should portray you as a problem-solver.

While this chapter covers ways to build an effective resume, its main goal is to help you perform better at the interview. You will achieve this as you evaluate your professional skills according to the exercises. In fact, you are likely to discover skills and achievements you didn't even know you had. A few you will use in your resume (merely a preview of coming attractions); the others you will use to knock 'em dead at the interview.

□ □ □

A good starting point is your current or last job title. Write it down. Then, jot down all the other different titles you have heard that describe this job. When you are finished, follow it with a three- or four-sentence description of your job functions. Don't think too hard about it, just do it. The titles and descriptions are not carved in stone. This written description is the beginning of the resume-building exercises. You'll be surprised at what you've written; it'll read better than you had thought.

All attributes that you discover and develop in the following exercises are valuable to an employer. You possess many desirable traits, and these exercises help to reveal and to package them.

□ *Exercise One:* Reread the written job description, then write down your most *important* duty/function. Follow this with a list of the skills or special training necessary to perform that duty. Next, list the achievements of which you are most proud in this area. It could look something like this:

> *Duty:* Train and motivate sales staff of six.
>
> *Skills:* Formal training skills. Knowledge of mar-

ket and ability to make untrained sales staff productive. Ability to keep successful salespeople
motivated and tied to the company.

Achievements: Reduced turnover seven percent;
increased sales 14 percent.

The potential employer is most interested in the achievements, those
things that make you stand out from the crowd. Try to appeal to a company's interests by conservatively estimating what your achievements
meant to your employer. If your achievements saved time, estimate how
much. If you saved money—how much? If your achievements made
money for the company, how much? Beware of exaggeration; if you
were part of a team, identify your achievements as such. It will make
your claims more believable and will demonstrate your ability to work
with others.

Achievements, of course, differ according to your profession. Most
of life's jobs fall into one of these broad categories:

- Sales
- Management and Administration
- Technical and Production

While it is usual to cite the differences between these major job functions, it is far more valuable to you to recognize the commonalities. In
sales, dollar volume is important In management or administration, the
parallel is time saved, which is money saved; saving money is just the
same as making money for your company. In the technical and production areas, increasing production (doing more in less time) accrues
exactly the same benefits to the company. Job titles may differ, yet all
employees have the same opportunity to benefit their employers, and in
turn, themselves.

The computer revolution of the seventies and the economic recession
in the early eighties have irrevocably changed the workplace. Today,
companies are doing more with less; they are leaner, have higher expectations of their employees, and plan to keep it that way. The people who
get hired and get ahead today are those with a basic understanding of
business goals. And successful job candidates are those who have the
best interests of the company and its profitability constantly in mind.

ercise Two: This simple exercise helps you get a clear picture of your achievements. If you were to meet with your supervisor to discuss a raise, what achievements would you want to discuss? List all you can think of, quickly. Then come back and flesh out the details.

☐ *Exercise Three:* This exercise is particularly valuable if you feel you can't see the forest for the trees.

> *Problem:* Think of a job-related problem you had to face in the last couple of years. Come on, everyone can remember a problem

> *Solution:* Describe your solution to this problem, step by step. List everything you did.

> *Results:* Finally, consider the results of your solution, in terms that would have value to an employer: money earned or saved; time saved.

☐ *Exercise Four:* Now, a valuable exercise that turns the absence of a negative into a positive. This one helps you look at your job in a different light and accents important but often overlooked areas that help make you special. Begin discovering for yourself some of the key personal traits that all companies look for.

First, consider actions that if not done properly would affect the goal of your job. If this is difficult, remember an incompetent co-worker. What did he or she do wrong? What did he or she do differently from *competent* employees?

Now, turn the absence of these negatives into positive attributes. For example, think of the employee who never managed to get to work on time. You could honestly say that someone who *did* come to work on time every day was punctual and reliable; believed in systems and procedures; was efficiency-minded and cost- and profit-conscious.

If you have witnessed the reprimands and ultimate termination of that tardy employee, they you will see the value of the *positive* traits in the eyes of an employer. The absence of negative traits makes you a desirable employee, but no one will know unless you tell them. On completion of the exercise, you will be able to make points about your background in a positive fashion. You will set yourself apart from others, if only because others do not understand the benefit of projecting all their positive attributes.

□ *Exercise Five:* Potential employers and interviewers are always interested in people who:

- Are efficiency-minded;

- Have an eye for economy;

- Follow procedures;

- Are profit-oriented.

Proceed through your work history and identify the aspects of your background that exemplify these traits. These newly discovered personal pluses will not only be woven into your resume, but will be reflected in the posture of your answers when you get to the interview.

□ □ □

You now need to take some of this knowledge and package it in a resume. There are three standard types of resumes:

Chronological: The most frequently used format. Use it when your work history is stable and your professional growth is consistent. Avoid it if you have experienced performance problems or have made frequent job changes.

Functional: Use this type if you have been unemployed for long periods of time or have jumped jobs too frequently. A functional resume is created without employment dates or company names, and concentrates on skills and responsibilities.

Prioritized: The prioritized resume can be useful if you have changed careers, or when current responsibilities don't relate specifically to the job you want. It is written with the most relevant experience to the job you're seeking placed first.

Notice that each style is designed to minimize certain undesirable traits. As few of us are perfect (present company excepted), most people find it most effective to create a combination resume.

Employers are wary of the "too-perfect" resume. With this in mind, there are just seven rules for creating a workmanlike resume.

☐ *Rule One:* Use the most general of job titles. You are, after all, a hunter of interviews, not of specific titles. Cast you net wide. Use a title that is specific enough to put you in the field, yet vague enough to elicit further questions. A job title can be made specifically vague by adding the term "specialist" (e.g., Computer Specialist, Administration Specialist, Production Specialist).

☐ *Rule Two:* Avoid giving a job objective. If you must state a specific job as your goal, couch it in terms of contributions you can make in that position. Do not state what you expect of the employer.

☐ *Rule Three:* Do not state your current salary. If you are earning too little or too much, you could rule yourself out before getting your foot in the door. Do not mention your desired salary for the same reason.

☐ *Rule Four:* Remember that people get great joy from getting pleasant surprises. Show a little gold now, but let the interviewer discover the motherlode at the interview.

☐ *Rule Five:* Take whatever steps necessary to keep the resume's length to a two-page maximum. No one reads long resumes; they are boring, and every company is frightened that if it lets in a windbag, it will never get him or her out again.

☐ *Rule Six:* Your resume must be typed. As a rule of thumb, three pages of double-spaced, handwritten notes make one page of typescript.

☐ *Rule Seven:* Finally, emphasize your achievements and problem-solving skills. Keep the resume general.

3.
The Executive Briefing

A general resume does have drawbacks. First, it is too general to relate your qualifications to each specific job. Second, more than one person will probably be interviewing you, and that is a major stumbling block. While you will ultimately report to one person, you may well be interviewed by other team members. When this happens, the problems begin.

A manager says, "Spend a few minutes with this candidate and tell me what you think." Your general resume may be impressive, but the manager rarely adequately outlines the job being filled or the specific qualifications he or she is looking for. This means that other interviewers do not have any way to qualify you fairly and specifically. While the manager will be looking for specific skills relating to projects at hand, personnel will be trying to match your skills to the job-description-manual vagaries, and the other interviewers will flounder in the dark because no one told them what to look for. This naturally could reduce your chances of landing a job offer.

Professionals in the employment services industry face this problem daily. At Dunhill we came up with a solution called the Executive Briefing. It enables you to quickly customize your resume to each specific job, and acts as a focusing device for whoever interviews you.

many great ideas, the Executive Briefing is beautiful in its sim-
It is a sheet of paper with the company's requirements for the
job opening listed on the left side, and your skills—matching point by
point the company's needs—on the right. It looks like this:

Executive Briefing

Dear Sir/Madam:

While my resume will provide you with a general outline of my work history,
my problem-solving abilities, and some achievements, I have taken the time to
list your current specific requirements and my applicable skills in those areas.
I hope this will enable you to use your time effectively today.

Your Requirements:	My Skills:
1. Management of public library service area (for circulation, reference, etc.).	1. Experience as head reference librarian at University of Smithtown.
2. Supervision of 14 full-time support employees.	2. Supervised support staff of 17.
3. Ability to work with larger supervisory team in planning, budgeting, and policy formulating.	3. During my last year, I was responsible for budget and reformation of circulation rules.
4. ALA-accredited MLS.	4. I have this degree.
5. 3 years' experience.	5. 1 year with public library; 2 with University of Smithtown.

This briefing assures that each resume you send out addresses the
job's specific needs and that every interviewer at that company will be
interviewing you for the same job.

Send an Executive Briefing with every resume; it will substantially increase your chances of obtaining an interview with the company. An
Executive Briefing sent with a resume provides a comprehensive picture
of a thorough professional, plus a personalized, fast, and easy-to-read
synopsis that details exactly how you can help with their current needs.

The use of an Executive Briefing is naturally restricted to jobs that you
have discovered through your own efforts or seen advertised. It is ob-

viously not appropriate for sending when the requirements of a specific job are unavailable. However, by following the directions in the next chapter, you will be able to use it frequently and effectively.

II

Getting
to
Square One

With the grunt work completed, you are loaded for bear and ready to knock 'em dead. So how do you begin?

What are your choices? Read the want ads? Everybody else does. Apply for jobs listed with the unemployment office? Everybody else does. Send resumes to companies on the off-chance they have a job that fits your resume? Everybody else does. Or, of course, you can wait for someone to call you. Employ these tactics as your main thrust for hunting down the best jobs in town, and you will fail as do *millions* of other people who fall into the trap of using such outdated job-hunting techniques.

When you look like a penguin, act like a penguin, and hide among penguins, don't be surprised if you get lost in the flock. Today's business marketplace demands a different approach. Your career does not take care of itself; you must go out and grab the opportunities. Grant yourself the right to pick and choose among *many* job offers with a guaranteed approach: pick up the telephone. "Hello, Mr. Smith? My name is Martin Yate. I am an experienced training specialist. . . ."

It's as easy as that.

Guide you destiny by speaking directly to the professionals who make their living in the same way you do. A few minutes spent calling different companies from your research dossier, and you will have an interview. When you get one interview from making a few calls, how many do you think could be arranged with a day's concerted effort?

Because you are in control, it is possible to set your multiple interviews close together. This way your interviewing skills improve from one to the next. And soon, instead of scheduling multiple interviews, you can be weighing multiple job offers.

4.
Paint
the Perfect Picture
on the Phone

Before making that first, nerve-racking telephone call, you must be prepared to achieve one of these three goals. They are listed in their priority.

- I will arrange a meeting; or

- I will arrange a time to talk further on the phone; or

- I will establish a referral lead on a promising job opening elsewhere.

Always keep these goals in mind. By the time you finish the next four chapters, you'll be able to make any one of them quickly and easily.

To make the initial phone call a success, all you need to do is paint a convincing word picture of yourself. To start, remember the old saying: "No one really listens; we are all just waiting for our turn to speak." With this in mind, you shouldn't expect to hold anyone's attention for extended periods of time, so the picture you create needs to be brief yet thorough. Most of all, it should be "specifically vague": specific enough to arouse interest, to make the company representative prick up his or her ears; vague enough to encourage questions, to make him or her *pursue* you. The aim is to paint a representation of your skills in broad brush strokes with examples of the money-making, money-saving, or time-saving accomplishments all companies like to hear about.

A presentation made over the telephone must possess four characteristics to be successful. These can best be remembered by an old acronym from the advertising world, AIDA.

- A—You must get the company representative's *attention.*

- I—You must get the company representative's *interest.*

- D—You must create a *desire* to know more about you.

- A—You must encourage the company representative to take *action.*

With AIDA you get noticed. The interest you generate will be displayed by questions being asked. "How much are you making?" or, "Do you have a degree?" or, "How many years' experience do you have?" By giving the appropriate answers to these and other questions (which will be discussed in detail), you will change interest into a desire to meet you and parlay that desire into an interview.

The types of questions you are asked also enable you to identify the company's specific needs, and once they are identified, you can gear the on-going conversation toward those needs.

Here are the steps in building your AIDA presentation:

☐ *Step One:* This covers who you are and what you do. It is planned to get the company representative's attention, to give the person a reason to stay on the phone. This introduction will include your job title and a brief generalized description of your duties and responsibilities. Use a non-specific job title, as you did for your resume. Remember: getting a foot in the door with a generalized title can provide the occasion to sell your superior skills.

Tell just enough about yourself to whet the company's appetite, and cause the representative to start asking questions. Again, keep your description a little vague. For example, if you describe yourself as simply "experienced," the company representative *must* try to qualify your statement with a question: "How much experience do you have?" That way, you establish a level of interest. *But,* if you describe yourself as having four years' experience, and the company is looking for seven, you are likely to be ruled out without even knowing there was a job to be filled. *Never* specify exact experience or list all your accomplishments during the initial presentation. Your aim is just to open a dialogue.

> *Example:*
> "Good morning, Mr. Smith. My name is Jenny Jones. I am an experienced office equipment salesperson with an in-depth knowledge of the office products industry. Have I caught you at a good time?"

Note: Never *ever* ask if you have caught someone at a *bad* time. You are offering them an excuse to say "yes." By the same token, asking whether you have caught someone at a good time will *usually* get you a "yes." Then you can go directly into the rest of your presentation.

☐ *Step Two:* Now you are ready to generate interest, and from that, desire; it's time to sell one or two of your accomplishments. You already should have identified these during the resume-building exercises. Pull out no more than two items and follow your introductory sentence with them. Keep them brief and to the point, without embellishments.

> *Example:*
> "As the #3 salesperson in my company, I increased sales in my territory 15 percent to over $1 million. In the last six months, I won three major accounts from my competitors."

☐ *Step Three:* You have made the company representative want to know more about you, so now you can make him or her take action. Include the reason for your call and a request to meet. It should be care-dully constructed to finish with a question that will bring a positive response, which will launch the two of you into a nuts-and-bolts discussion between two professionals:

Example:
"The reason I'm calling, Mr. Smith, is that I'm looking for a new challenge, and having researched your company, I felt we might have some areas for discussion. Are these the types of skills and accomplishments you look for in your staff?"

Your presentation ends with a question that guarantees a positive response, and the conversation gets moving.

□ □ □

Your task now is to write out a presentation using these guidelines and your work experience. Knowing exactly what you are going to say and what you wish to achieve is the only way to generate multiple interviews and multiple job offers. When your presentation is prepared and written, read it aloud to yourself, and imagine the faceless company representative on the other end of the line. Practice with a friend or spouse.

After you make the actual presentation on the phone, you'll *really* begin to work on arranging a meeting, another phone conversation, or establishing a referral. There will likely be a silence on the other end after your initial pitch. Be patient. The company representative needs time to digest your words. If you feel tempted to break the silence, resist; you do not want to break the person's train of thought, nor do you want the ball back in your court.

This contemplative silence may last as long as 20 seconds, but when the company representative responds, there will be only three things that can happen:

1. *Company representative can agree with you and arrange a meeting.*

2. *Company representative can ask questions that show interest.*

   Examples:
   ● Do you have a degree?

   ● How much are you earning?

Any question, because it denotes interest, is known as a *buy signal.*

And handled properly, it will enable you to arrange a meeting.

3. Company representative can raise an objection.

> *Examples:*
> ● I don't need anyone like that now.
>
> ● Send me a resume.

These objections, when handled properly, will *also* result in an interview with the company, or at least a referral to someone else who has job openings. In fact, you will frequently find that objections prove themselves to be terrific opportunities disguised as unsolvable problems.

I hope you can handle the first option with little assistance, because for obvious reasons, it doesn't get a chapter; you can go straight to section III. The next two chapters focus on buy signals and objections, and how to turn them into interviews.

5.
Responding to
Buy Signals

With just a touch of nervous excitement you finish your presentation: "Are these the types of skills and accomplishments you look for in your staff?" There is silence on the other end. It is broken by a question. You breathe a sigh of relief because you remember that *any* question denotes interest and is a *buy signal.*

Now, conversation is a two-way street, and you are most likely to win an interview when you take responsibility for your half of the conversatior Just as the employer's questions show interest in you, your questions should show your interest in the work done at the company. By asking questions of your own in the normal course of that chat, questions usually tagged on to the end of one of your answers, you will forward the conversation. Also, these questions help you find out what particular skills and qualities are important to each different employer. Inquisitiveness will increase your knowledge of the opportunity at hand, and that knowledge will give you the power to arrange a meeting.

The alternative is to leave all the interrogation to the employer. That will place you on the defensive and at the end of the talk, you will be as ignorant of the real job parameters as you were at the start. And the employer will know less about you than you might want him to know.

Applying the technique of giving a short answer and finishing each reply with a question will carry your call to its logical conclusion: the interviewer will tell you the job specifics, and as that happens, you will present the relevant skills or attributes. In any conversation, the person who asks the questions controls its outcome. You called the employer to get an interview as the first step in generating a job offer, so take control of your destiny by taking control of the conversation.

> *Example:*
>
> *Jenny Jones:* "Good morning, Mr. Smith. My name is Jenny Jones. I am an experienced office equipment salesperson with an in-depth knowledge of the office products industry. Have I caught you at a good time? . . . As the #3 salesperson in my company, I increased sales in my territory 15 percent to over $1 million. In the last six months, I won three major accounts from my competitors. The reason I'm calling, Mr. Smith, is that I'm looking for a new challenge, and having researched your company, I felt we might have areas for discussion. Are these the types of skills and accomplishments you look for in your staff?"
>
> *[Pause.]*
>
> *Mr. Smith:* "Yes, they are. What type of equipment have you been selling?" *[Buy signal!]*
>
> *J:* "My company carries a comprehensive range, and I sell both the top and bottom of the line, according to my customers' needs. I have been noticing a considerable interest in the new multi-function machines. *[You've made it a conversation; you further it with the following . . .]* Has that been your experience recently?"
>
> *S:* "Yes, especially in the color and acetate capability machines. *[Useful information for you.]* Do you have a degree?" *[Buy signal!]*
>
> *J:* "Yes, I do. *[Just enough information to keep the company representative chasing you.]* I understand your company prefers degreed salespeople to deal with its more sophisticated clients." *[Your research is paying off.]*

S: "Our customer base is very sophisticated, and they expect certain behavior and competence from us. *[An inkling of the kind of person they want to hire.]* How much experience do you have?" *[Buy signal!]*

J: "Well, I've worked in both operations and sales, so I have a wide experience base. *[General but thorough.]* How many years of experience are you looking for?" *[Turning it around, but furthering the conversation.]*

S: "Ideally, four or five for the position I have in mind. *[More good information.]* How many do you have?" *[Buy signal!]*

J: "I have two with this company, and one and a half before that. I fit right in with your needs, don't you agree?" *[How can Mr. Smith say no?]*

S: "Uhmmm . . . what's your territory?" *[Buy signal!]*

J: "I cover the metropolitan area. Mr. Smith, it really *does* sound as if we might have something to talk about. *[Remember, your first goal is the face-to-face interview.]* I am planning to take Thursday and Friday off at the end of the week. Can we meet then? *[Make Mr. Smith decide what day he can see you, rather than whether he will see you at all.]* Which would be best for you?"

S: "How about Friday morning? Can you bring a resume?"

Your conversation should proceed with this give-and-take. Your questions show interest, carry the conversation forward, and teach you more about the company's needs. By the end of the conversation you have an interview arranged and several key areas to promote when you arrive:

● Company sees growth in multi-function machines, especially those with color and acetate capabilities

● They want business and personal sophistication

- They ideally want four or five years' experience

- They are interested in your metropolitan contacts

The above is a fairly simple scenario, and even though it is constructive, it doesn't show you the tricky buy signals that can spell disaster in your job hunt. They are *apparently* simple buy signals, yet in reality they are a part of every interviewer's arsenal called "knock-out" questions— questions that can save the interviewer time by quickly ruling out certain types of candidates. Although these questions most frequently arise during the initial telephone conversation, they can crop up at the face-to-face interview; the answering techniques are applicable throughout the interview cycle.

Note: We all come from different backgrounds and geographical areas. I see and recognize these regional differences every day in my training job. So understand that while my answers cover correct approaches and responses, they do not attempt to capture the rich regional and personal flavor of conversation. You and I will never talk alike. So, don't learn the example answers parrot-fashion. Instead, you should take the essence of the responses and personalize them until the words fall easily from your lips.

□

Buy Signal: "How much are you making/do you want?"

This is a direct question looking for a direct answer, yet it is a knock-out question. Earning either too little or too much could ruin your chances before you're given the opportunity to shine in person. There are a number of options that could serve you better than a direct answer.

□ *Put yourself above the money:* "I'm looking for a job and a company to call home. If I am the right person for you, I'm sure you'll make me a fair offer. What is the salary range for the position?"

□ *Give a vague answer:* "In the 20s. The most important things to me are the job itself and the company. What is the salary range for the position?"

☐ *Or you could use a technique employed by most salespeople, and answer a question with a question:* "How much does the job pay?" It is sometimes very effective to answer a question with a question; if you don t feel yourself to be the sales type, however, you may neea to practice it.

When you are pressed a second time for an exact dollar figure, be honest and forthright. You have to be. If it turns out to be too much, say, "Mr. Smith, my previous employers felt I am well worth the money I earn due to my skills, dedication, and honesty. Were we to meet, I'm sure I could demonstrate my value and my ability to contribute to your department. You'd like an opportunity to make that evaluation, wouldn't you?"

Notice the "wouldn't you?" at the end of the reply. A reflexive question such as this is a great conversation-forwarding technique because it encourages a positive response. Conservative use of reflexive questions can really help you move things along. Watch the sound of your voice, though. A reflexive question can sound pleasantly conversational or pointed and accusatory; it's a case of not *what* you say, but *how* you say it. These questions are easy to create. Just add, "wouldn't you?", "didn't you?", "won't you?", "couldn't you?", "shouldn't you?", or "don't you?" to the end of any sentence and the interviewer will almost always answer "yes." You have kept the conversation alive.

Repeat the reflexive questions to yourself. They have a certain rhythm that will help you remember them.

☐

Buy Signal: "Do you have a degree?"

Always answer the exact question; beware of giving unreouested and possibly too much information. For example, if you have a bachelor's degree from NYU, your answer is "Yes," not "Yes, I have a bachelor's degree in fine arts from NYU." Perhaps the company wants an architecture degree. Perhaps the company representative has bad feelings about NYU graduates. You don't want to be knocked out before you've been given the chance to prove yourself.

"Yes, I have a degree. What background are you looking for?"

You can always answer a question with a question. "I have a diverse educational background. Ideally, what are you looking for?"

If a degree that you lack is required, strive to use the "Life University" answer. For instance: "My education was cut short by the necessity of earning a living at an early age. My past managers have found that my life experience and responsible attitude is a *very* valuable asset to the department. Also, I intend to return to school to continue my education."

□

Buy Signal: "How much experience do you have?"

Too much or too little could easily rule you out. Be careful how you answer and try to gain time. It is a vague question, and you have a right to ask for qualifications.

"Could you help me with that question?" or, "Are you looking for overall experience or in some specific areas?" or, "Which areas are most important to you?" Again, you answer a question with a question. The employer's response to this, while gaining you time, tells you what it takes to do the job and therefore what you have to say to get it, so take mental notes (you can even write them down, if you have time). Then give an appropriate response.

You might want to retain control of the conversation by asking another question, for example, "The areas of expertise you require sound very interesting, and it sounds as if you have some exciting projects at hand. Exactly what projects would I be involved with over the first several months?"

After one or two buy signal questions are asked (apart from the ones mentioned, they contain no traps), you should ask to meet the company. If you simply ask, "Would you like to meet me?" there are only two possible responses: yes or no. Your options are greatly lessened. However, when you intimate that you will be in the area on a particular date or dates ("I'm going to be in town on Thursday and Friday, Ms. Smith. Which would be better for you?"), you have asked a question that moves the conversation along dramatically. This question gives the company representative the choice of meeting you on Thursday or Friday, rather than meeting you or not meeting you. By presuming the "yes," you reduce the chances of hearing a negative, and increase the possibility of a face-to-face meeting.

6.
Responding to Objections

Even with the most convincing word picture, the silence may not be broken by a buy signal, but by an objection. An objection is usually a statement, not a question: "Why don't you send me a resume," or, "I don't have time to see you," or, "You are earning too much," or, "You'll have to talk to personnel," or, "I don't need anyone like you right now."

These seem like brush-off lines, but almost all objections can be parlayed into interviews when handled properly. Often they are just more disguised opportunities. As this section teaches you to seize hidden opportunities successfully, notice that all your responses have a commonality with buy signal responses: they all end with a question, a question that will enable you to learn more about the reason for the objection, overcome it, and once again lead the conversation toward a face-to-face interview.

In dealing with objections, as with differences of opinion, nothing is gained by confrontation, though much is to be gained by appreciation of the other's viewpoint. Most objections you hear are best handled by first demonstrating your understanding of the other's viewpoint. Always start your response with "I understand," or, "I can appreciate your position," or, "I see your point," or, "Of course," followed by,

"However . . . " or, "Also consider . . . " or a similar line that carries the conversation forward.

Remember, these responses should not be learned merely to be repeated. You need only to understand and implement their *meaning,* to understand their *concept* and put the answers in your own words. Personalize all the suggestions to your character and style of speech.

□

Objection: "Why don't you send me a resume?"

Danger here. The company representative may be genuinely interested in seeing your resume as a first step in the interview cycle; or it may be a polite way of getting you off the phone. You should identify what the real reason is without causing antagonism. At the same time, you want to open up the conversation. A good reply would be: "Of course, Mr. Smith. Would you give me your exact title and the full address? . . . Thank you. So that I can be sure that my qualifications fit your needs, what skills are you looking for in this position?"

Notice the steps:

- Apparent agreement to start

- A show of consideration

- A question to guide the conversation at the end

Answering in this fashion will open up the conversation. Now, our hypothetical Mr. Smith will relay the aspects of the job that are important to him. With this knowledge, you can sell Smith on your skills over the phone. Also, you will be able to draw attention to your skills in these specific areas in the future, in:

- Following conversations

- The cover letter to your resume

- The executive briefing

- Your face-to-face meeting

- Your follow-up after the meeting

The information you glean will give you power and will increase your chances of receiving a job offer.

□

Objection: "I don't have time to see you."

If the employer is too busy to see you, he or she has a problem, and by recognizing that, perhaps you can show yourself as the one to solve it. However, you should avoid confrontation; it is important that you demonstrate empathy for the speaker. Agree, empathize, and ask a question that moves the conversation forward.

"I understand how busy you must be; it sounds like the kind of atmosphere I could work well in. Perhaps I could call you back at a better time. When are you least busy, the morning or afternoon?"

The company representative will either make time to talk now, or will arrange a better time for the two of you to talk further.

Here are three other wordings you could use for the same objection: "Since you are so busy, what is the best time of day for you? First thing in the morning, or is the afternoon a quieter time?" or, "I will be in your area tomorrow, so why don't I come by and see you?"

Or, of course, you can combine the two: "I'm going to be in your part of town tomorrow, and I could drop by and see you. What is your quietest time, morning or afternoon?" By presuming the invitation for a meeting, you make it harder for the company representative to object. And if he or she is *truly* busy, your consideration will make it even harder to object.

□

Objection: "You are earning too much."

You should not have brought up salary in the first place. Go straight to jail. If the client brought up the matter, that's a buy signal, which was discussed in the last chapter. If the job really doesn't pay enough, you got (as the carnival barker says) close, but no cigar! How to make a success of this seeming dead end is handled in the next chapter.

□

Objection: "We only promote from within."

Your response could be: "I realize that, Mr. Jones. Your development of employees is a major reason I want to get in! I am bright, conscientious, and need a company like yours. When you do hire from the outside, what assets are you looking for?"

The response finishes with a question designed to carry the conversation forward, and to give you a new opportunity to sell yourself. Notice that the response assumes that the company *is* hiring from the outside, even though the company representative has said otherwise. You have called his bluff, but in a professional, inoffensive manner.

☐

Objection: "You'll have to talk to personnel."

Your reply is: "Of course, Mr. Smith. Whom should I speak to in personnel and what specific position should I mention?"

You cover a good deal of ground with this response. You establish whether there is a job there or whether you are being fobbed off to personnel to waste their time and your own. Also, you move the conversation forward again, and have changed the thrust of it to your advantage. Develop a specific job-related question to ask while the company representative is answering the first question. It can open a fruitful line for you to pursue. If you receive a non-specific reply, probe a little deeper. A simple phrase like, "That's interesting, please tell me more," or, "Why's that?" will usually do the trick.

Or you can ask: "When I speak to personnel, will it be about a specific job *you* have, or is it to see if I might fill a position elsewhere in the company?"

Armed with this information, you can talk to personnel about your conversation with Mr. Smith. Remember to get the name of a specific person to speak with, and to quote the company representative.

> *Example:*
> "Good morning, Mr. Johnson. Mr. Smith, the regional sales manager, suggested we should speak to arrange an interview."

This way, you will show personnel that you are *not* a waste of their time; because you know someone in the company, you won't be regarded as one of the hundreds of blind-callers they always get. As the most overworked, understaffed department in a company, they will appreciate that. Most important, you will stand out, be noticed.

Don't look at the personnel department as a roadblock; it may contain a host of opportunities for you. Because a large company may have many different departments that can use your talents, personnel is likely to be the only department that knows all the openings. You might be able to arrange three or four interviews with the same company for three or four different positions!

☐

Objection: "I really wanted someone with a degree."

You could answer *this* by saying: "Mr. Smith, I appreciate your position. It was necessary that I start earning a living early in life. If we meet, I am certain you would recognize the value of my additional practical experience. All we would need is a short while, and I'm going to be in your area tomorrow and next week. When would be a good time for you?"

If that doesn't work, ask what the company policy is for support and encouragement of employees taking night classes, continuing education courses, etc.

☐

Objection: "I don't need anyone like you now."

Short of suggesting the employer fire someone to make room for you, chances of getting an interview with this particular company are slim, but with the right question, this person will give you a personal introduction to someone else who could use your talents. Asking that right question or series of questions is what networking and the next chapter are all about. So on the occasions when the techniques for answering buy signals or rebutting objections do not get you a meeting, "Getting Live Leads from Dead Ends" will!

7.
Getting Live Leads
From Dead Ends

There will be times when you have said all the right things on the phone, but hear, "I can't use anyone like you right now." Not every company has a job opening for you, nor are you right for every job. There will be times when you must accept a temporary setback and understand that the rejection is not one of you as a human being. By using other interview development questions, though, you will be able to turn these occasions into job interviews.

The company representative is a professional and knows other professionals in his or her field, in other departments, subsidiaries, even other companies. If you approach the phone presentation in a professional manner, he or she, as a fellow professional, will be glad to advise you on who is looking for someone with your skills. Nearly everyone you call will be pleased to head you in the right direction, *but only if you ASK!* And you'll be able to ask as many questions as you desire, because you will be recognized as a colleague intelligently using the professional network. The company representative knows also that his good turn in referring you to a friend at another company will be returned in future. And, as a general rule, companies prefer candidates to be referred this way over any other method.

But do *not* expect people to be clairvoyant. There are two sayings:

"You get what you ask for,"

and

"If you don't ask, you don't get."

When you are sure that no job openings exist within a particular company, *ask* one of these questions:

- "Who else in the company might need someone with my qualifications?"

- "Does your company have any other divisions or subsidiaries that might need someone with my attributes?"

- "Do you know anyone in the business community who might have a lead for me?"

- "What are the most rapidly growing companies in the area?"

- "Whom should I speak to there?"

- "Do you know anyone at the Corporation Company, Incorporated?"

- "When do you anticipate an opening in your company?"

- "Are you planning any expansion or new projects that might create an opening?"

- "Do you see any change in your manpower needs?"

Each one of these interview development questions can gain you an introduction or lead to a fresh opportunity. The questions have not been put in any order of importance. That is for you to do. Take a sheet of paper and, looking at the list, figure out what question you would ask if you had time to ask only one. Write it down. Do this with the remaining questions on the list. As you advance, a comfortable set of prioritized questions will be developed. Add questions of your own. For instance, the type of computer or word-processing equipment a company has might be important to some professions, but not to others, and a company representative might be able to lead you to companies that have your machines. Be sure that any question you add to your list is specific and leads to a job opening. Avoid questions like, "How's business these days?" Time is valuable, and time is money to both of you. When you're satisfied with your list of interview development questions, put them on a fresh sheet of paper and store it safely with your telephone presentation and resume.

These interview development questions will lead you to a substantial number of jobs in the hidden job market. You are getting referrals from the "in" crowd, who know who is hiring whom long before that news is generally known, and by so doing, you establish a very effective referral network.

When you get leads on companies and specific individuals to talk to, be sure to thank your benefactor and ask to use his or her name as an introduction. The answer, you will find, will always be "yes," but asking shows you as someone with manners, and in this day and age, that *alone* will set you apart. You might also suggest to your contact that you leave your telephone number in case he or she runs into someone who can use you. You will be surprised at how many people call back with a lead.

With personal permission to use someone's name on your next networking call, you have been given the greatest of job-search gifts: a personal introduction. In these instances, your call will begin with:

> "Hello, Mr. Smith. My name is Jack Jones. Joseph McDonald recommended I give you a call. By the way, he sends his regards." *(Pause for any response to this.)* "He felt we might have something valuable to discuss."

Follow up on every lead you get. Too many people become elated at securing an interview for themselves and then cease all effort to generate additional interviews, believing a job offer is definitely on its way. Your goal is to have a choice of the best jobs in town, and without multiple interviews, there is no way you'll have that choice. Asking interview development questions ensures that you are tapping all the secret recesses of the hidden job market.

Networking is a continuous cycle:

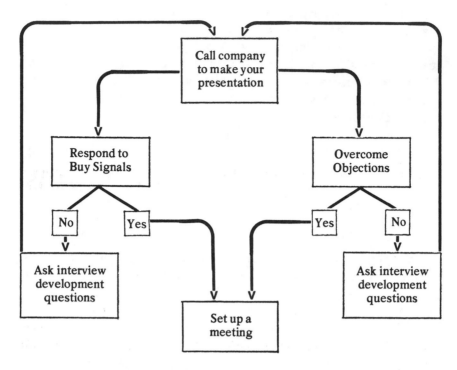

Make a commitment to sell yourself, to make telephone calls, to make a referral network, to recognize buy signals and objections for what they really are—opportunities to shine. Make a commitment to ask interview development questions at every seeming dead end: they will lead you to every job in town.

8.
The Telephone Interview

In this glorious technological age, the first contact with a potential employer is always by telephone. It's the way business is done today.

It happens in one of three ways:

- When you are networking, and the company representative goes into a screening process immediately because you have aroused his or her interest;

- a company calls unexpectedly as a result of a resume you have mailed, and catches you off-guard;

- or you or an agency you have spoken to has set up a specific time for a telephone interview.

Whatever circumstance creates this telephone interview, you must be prepared to handle the questioning and use every means at your disposal to win the real thing—the *face-to-face* meeting. The telephone interview is the trial run for the face-to-face, and is an opportunity not to be bumbled; your happiness and prosperity may hinge on it.

his, the first contact with your future employer, will test your mental preparation. Remember: you can plant in your mind any thought, any plan, desire, strategy, or purpose, and translate it into reality. Put your goal down on paper and read it aloud to yourself every day, because the constant reiteration will crystallize your aims, and that provides the most solid base of preparation.

Being prepared for a telephone interview takes organization. You never know when a company is going to call once you have started networking (the word gets around), although it is usually at the worst of times, such as 8 o'clock Monday morning when you are sleeping late, or 4:56 in the afternoon, just as you return from walking the dog. You can avoid being caught *completely* off-guard by keeping your resume and alphabetized company dossiers by the telephone.

The most obvious (and often most neglected) point to remember is this: during the interview, the company representative has only ears with which to judge you. This is something you must overcome. Here are some tips:

☐ *Take a surprise call in stride.* If you receive a call as a result of a mailed resume or a telephone message you left, and you are unprepared, be calm. Sound positive, friendly, and collected:

> "Thank you for calling, Mr. Smith. How do you
> spell that? Would you wait just a moment while I
> close the door?"

Put the phone down, take three deep breaths to slow your heart down, pull out the appropriate company dossier and your resume, put a smile on your face (it improves the timbre of your voice), and pick up the phone again. Now you are in control of yourself and the situation.

☐ *Beware of over-familiarity.* You should always refer to the interviewer by his or her surname until invited to do otherwise.

☐ *Allow the company representative to do most of the talking, to ask the questions.*

☐ *Beware of giving yes/no answers.* They give no real information about your abilities.

☐ *Be factual in your answers.* Brief yet thorough.

☐ *Keep up your end of the conversation.* Don't let the interviewer do *all* the talking. Ask some questions of your own.

☐ *Speak directly into the telephone.* Keep the mouthpiece about 1 inch from your mouth. Do not smoke or eat while on the phone. Numbered among the mystical properties of our telephone system is its excellence at picking up and amplifying background music and voices, especially young ones. This is only excelled by the power with which it transmits the sounds of food or gum being chewed or smoke being inhaled or exhaled. Smokers, remember: there are no laws about discriminating against smokers, and therefore, all non-smokers naturally discriminate. They know that even if you don't smoke at the interview, you'll have been chain-smoking before and will carry the smell with you as long as you are around them. So, they won't even give you a chance to get through the door.

☐ *Take notes.* They will be invaluable to you in preparing for the face-to-face meeting. Were it not for the recent furor over the clandestine use of tape recorders, I would have recommended that you buy a cheap tape recorder and a phone attachment (from your local electronics store) and tape the whole conversation.

If, for any reason, the company representative is interrupted, jot down the topic under discussion. When he or she gets back on the line, you helpfully recap: "We were just discussing . . . " This will be appreciated, and will set you apart from the others.

The company representative may talk about the corporation, and from the dossier in front of you, you will also know facts about the outfit. A little flattery goes a long way: admire the company's achievements and you are, in fact, admiring the interviewer. Likewise, if any areas of common interest arise, comment on them, and agree with the interviewer when it is possible; people hire people like themselves.

If the interviewer does not give you the openings you need to sell yourself, be ready to salvage the situation and turn it to your advantage. Have a few work-related questions prepared (e.g., "What exactly will be the three major responsibilities in this job?" or, "Would I be using a personal computer?''). While you are getting the explanation, wait for a pause so that you can tell the interviewer your appropriate skills: "Would it be of value if I described my experience in the area of office management?" or, "Then my experience in word processing should be a great help to you." Under no circumstances, though, should you ask about the money you want, or benefits and vacation time; that comes later.

Remember that your single objective at this point is to sell yourself and your skills; if you don't do that, you may never get the face-to-face interview.

The telephone interview has come to an end when you are asked whether you have any questions. Ask any more questions that will improve your understanding of the job requirements. If you haven't asked before, now is the time to establish what projects you would be working on in the first six months. By discovering them now, you will have time before the face-to-face meeting to package your skills to the needs at hand, and to create the appropriate Executive Briefing.

And if you have not already asked or been invited to meet the interviewer, now is the time. Take the initiative.

"It sounds like a very interesting opportunity, Ms./Mr. Smith, and a situation where I could definitely make a contribution. The most pressing question I have now is, when can we get together?" [*Note:* Even though the emphasis throughout has been on putting things in your own words, *do* use "make a contribution." It shows pride in your work—a key personal trait.]

Once the details are confirmed, finish with this request: "If I need any additional information before the interview, I would like to feel free to get back to you." The company representative will naturally agree. No matter how many questions you get answered in the initial conversation, there will always be something you forget. This allows you to call again to satisfy any curiosity and will also enable you to increase rapport. Don't take *too* much advantage of this, though. One well-placed phone call that contains two or three considered questions will be appreciated; four or five phone calls will not.

Taking care to ascertain the correct spelling and pronunciation of the interviewer's name shows your concern for the small but important things in life: it *will* be noticed. This is also a good time to establish who else will be interviewing you, their titles and how long the meeting is expected to last. Follow with a casual inquiry as to what direction the meeting will take.

"Would you tell me some of the critical areas we will discuss on Thursday?" you might ask. The knowledge gained will go a distance in packaging yourself and will allow you time to bone up on any weak or rusty areas.

It is difficult to evaluate an opportunity properly over the telephone. Even if the job doesn't sound right, go to the interview. It will give you practice, and the job may look better when you have more facts. You might even discover a more suitable opening when you go to the face-to-face interview.

9.
The Curtain Goes Up

Backstage in the theater, the announcement, "Places, please," is made five minutes before the curtain goes up. This is the performers' signal to psyche themselves up, complete final costume adjustments, and make time to reach the stage. They are getting ready to go onstage and knock 'em dead. You should go through a similar process.

Winning that job offer depends not only on the things you do well, but also on the absence of things you do poorly. As the interview date approaches, settle down with your resume and the exercises you performed in building it. Immerse yourself in your past successes and strengths. This is a time for building confidence. A little nervousness is perfectly natural and healthy, but channel the extra energy in a positive direction by beginning your physical and mental preparations. First, you should assemble your interview kit. It will include:

☐ *The company dossier.*

☐ *Two or three copies of your resume, all but one for the interviewer.* It is perfectly all right to have it in front of you at the interview; it shows you are organized. It also makes a great cheat sheet (after all, the interviewer is using it for that reason) and it can be kept on your lap during the interview with pad and pencil. It is not unusual to hear, "Mr. Jones wasn't hired because he didn't pay attention to detail and could not even remember his employment dates." And those are just the kinds of things you are likely to forget in the heat of the moment.

☐ *A pad of paper and writing instruments.* These articles have a two-fold purpose. They demonstrate your organization and interest in the job; they also give you something constructive to do with your hands during the interview. Bring along a blue or black pen for filling out applications.

☐ *Contact telephone numbers.* If you get detained on the way to the interview, you can call and let the company representative know.

☐ *Take the sensible precaution of gathering reference letters from your employers, just in case.*

☐ *A list of job-related questions.* During the interview is the time when you gather information to evaluate a job (the actual evaluation comes when you have an offer in hand). At the end of the interview, you will be given the opportunity to ask additional questions. Develop some that help you understand the job's parameters and potential. You might ask:

- Why is the job open?

- Where does the job lead?

- What is the job's relationship to other departments?

- How do the job and the department relate to the corporate mission?

Now you have a little more work to do:

☐ *Gather any additional information you can about the company or the job.* If time permits, ask the interviewer's secretary to send you some company literature. Absorb whatever you can.

☐ *Make sure you have directions to the interview.* Decide on your form of transportation and finalize your time of departure. Check the route, distance, and travel time. Write all this down legibly and put it with the rest of your interview kit. If you forget to verify date, time, and place (including floor and suite number), you might not even arrive at the right place, or on the right day, for your interview.

First impressions are the strongest you make, and they are based on your appearance. There is only one way to dress for the first meeting: clean-cut and conservative. You may or may not see yourself this way, but how you see yourself is not important now; your only concern is how others see you. As you could be asked to appear for an interview at a scant couple of hours notice, you must be in a constant state of readiness. Keep your best two suits of clothing freshly cleaned, shirts ironed, and shoes polished. Never wear these outfits unless you are interviewing. Here are some more tips:

- Regardless of sex or hairstyle, take it to the lawn doctor once a month.

- Keep jewelry to a minimum. Wedding band is acceptable, of course.

- While a shower or bath prior to an interview is most desirable, the wearing of aftershave or perfume is most decidedly not. You are trying to get *hired*, not dated.

- You should never drink alcohol the day before an interview. It affects eyes, skin pallor, and your wits.

- Nails should be trimmed and manicured at all times, even if you work with your hands.

For women:

- Wear a suit or a dress with a jacket. Do not wear pants.

- If you carry a briefcase, don't carry a purse. You may meet a number of people and will have trouble juggling your luggage to shake hands.

- Wear low heels. Spike heels make you wobble

and are regarded by many as inappropriate in the workplace.

- Avoid linen; it fatigues too easily.

- Stay away from everything low-cut, tight, or diaphanous.

For men:

- Avoid loud colors and anything that has been faddish. . . .

- . . . such as that Hawaiian tie. A 2½" to 2¾" tie is *de rigueur*. Patterns should be paisley or foulard. Avoid anything wider unless you are applying for a job as a carpet salesman.

- Blue or gray for suits primarily. White for shirts is always safest.

- Black shoes with plain socks.

The way you dress, the way you look to a potential employer at the first interview, tells him or her how you feel about yourself. It also portrays how seriously you take both the interview and the interviewer.

□ □ □

To arrive at an interview too early indicates over-anxiousness; to arrive late is inconsiderate. The only sensible solution is to arrive at the interview on time, but at the location early. This allows you time to visit the restroom and make the necessary adjustments to your appearance. Take a couple of minutes in this temporary sanctuary to perform your final mental preparations:

- Review the company dossier.

- Recall the positive things you will say about past employers.

- Breathe deeply and slowly for a minute. This will dispel your natural physical tension.

- Repeat to yourself that the interview will be a success and afterwards the company representatives will wonder how they ever managed without you.

- Smile and head for the interview.

Under no circumstances back out because you do not like the receptionist or the look of the office; that would be allowing interview nerves to get the better of you. As you are shown into the office, you are on!

This potential new employer wants an aggressive and dynamic employee, but someone who is less aggressive and dynamic than themselves, so take your lead from the interviewer.

Do:

- Give a firm handshake; one shake is enough.

- Make eye contact and smile. Say, "Hello, Ms. Smith. I am John Jones. I have been looking forward to meeting you."

Do not:

- Use first names (unless asked).

- Smoke (even if invited).

- Sit down (until invited).

- Show anxiety or boredom.

- Look at your watch.

- Discuss equal rights, sex, race, national origin, religion, age.

- Show samples of your work (unless requested).

- Ask about benefits, salary, vacation.

- Assume a submissive role; treat the interviewer with respect, but as an equal.

Now you are ready for anything. Except for the tough questions that are going to be thrown at you next.

III

Great Answers to Tough Interview Questions

"Like being on trial for your life" is how many people look at a job interview. They are probably right. With the interviewer as judge and jury, you are at least on trial for your livelihood. Therefore, you must lay the foundation for a winning defense. F. Lee Bailey, America's most celebrated defense attorney, attributes his success in the courtroom to preparation. He likens himself to a magician going into court with 50 rabbits in his hat, not knowing which one he'll really need, and ready to pull out any single one. Bailey is successful because he is ready for any eventuality. He takes the time to analyze every situation and every possible option. He never underestimates his opposition. He is always prepared. F. Lee Bailey usually wins.

Another famous attorney, Louis Nizer, successfully defended *all* of his 50-plus capital offense clients. When lauded as the greatest courtroom performer of his day, Nizer denied the accolade. He claimed for himself the distinction of being the *best prepared.*

You won't win your day in court just based on your skills. As competition for the best jobs increases, employers are comparing more and more applicants for every opening and asking more and more questions. To win against stiff competition, you need more than just your merits. When the race is close, the final winner is often as not picked for a comparative lack of negatives when ranged against the other contenders. Like Bailey and Nizer, you can prove to yourself that the job always goes to the best prepared.

During an interview, employers ask you dozens of searching questions: questions that test your confidence, poise, and desirable personality traits. Questions that trick you into contradicting yourself, and questions that probe your quick thinking and job skills. They are all designed so that the interviewer can make decisions in four critical areas: Can you do the job? Do you fit the company image? Will you complement or disrupt the department? Is the money right?

Notice that only one of the critical areas has anything to do with your professional skills. Being able to do the job is only part-way to getting an offer. Whether you will fit in and make a contribution is just as important to the interviewer. Those traits the company probes for during the interview are the same that will mark a person for professional growth when on board. In this era of high unemployment and high specialization, companies become more critical in the selection process and look more actively for certain traits, some of which cannot be ascertained by a direct question or answer. Consequently, the interviewer will seek a pattern in your replies that shows your possession of these traits.

The time spent in "court" on trial for your livelihood contains four deadly traps:

- Failure to listen to the question.

- Annoying the interviewer by answering a question that was not asked.

- Providing superfluous information (keep answers brief, thorough, and to the point).

- Attempting to interview without preparation.

The effect of these blunders is cumulative, and each reduces your chances of receiving a job offer.

The number of offers you win in your search for the ideal job depends on your ability to answer a staggering array of questions in terms that have value and relevance to the employer: "Why do you want to work here?" or, "What are your biggest accomplishments?" or, "How long will it take you to make a contribution?" or, "Why should I hire you?" or, "What can you do for us that someone else cannot do?" or, "What is your greatest weakness?" or, "Why aren't you earning more?" or, "What interests you least about this job?" are just *some* of the questions you will be asked.

The example answers in the following chapters come from across the job spectrum. While the example answer might come from the mouth of an administrator—and you are a salesperson—the commonality of all job functions in contributing to the bottom line will help you draw the parallel to *your* job.

You will also notice that each of the example answers teaches a small, yet valuable lesson in good business behavior; something you can use both to get the job and to make a good impression when you are on board.

And remember, the answers provided in the following chapters should not be repeated word for word, exactly as they come off the page. *You* have your own style of speech (not to mention your own kind of business experience), so try to put the answers in your *own* words.

10.
How to
Knock 'em Dead

Can you answer all these questions off the top of your head? Can you do it in a way that will set your worth above the other job candidates? I doubt it; they were *designed* to catch you off guard. But they won't after you have read this book.

Even if you could answer some of them, it would not be enough to assure you of victory: the employer is looking for certain intangible assets as well. Think back to your last job for a moment. Can you recall someone with fewer skills, less professionalism, and less dedication who somehow leveraged his or her career into a position of superiority to you? He or she was able to do this only by cleverly projecting a series of personality traits that are universally sought by all successful companies. Building these key traits into your answers to the interviewer's questions will win you any job and set the stage for your career growth at the new company.

There are 20 key personality traits; they are the passport to your success at an interview. Use them for reference as you customize your answers to this chapter's tough questions.

□ □ □

Personal Profile:

Personal profile keys are searched for by the interviewer to determine what type of person you *really* are. The presence of these keys in your answers tells the company representative how you feel about yourself, your chosen career, and what you will be like to work with. Few of these keys will arise from direct questions. Your future employer will be searching for them in your answers to specific job performance probes. The following words and phrases are those you will project as part of your successful, healthy personal profile:

> *Drive:* A desire to get things done. Goal-oriented.

> *Motivation:* Enthusiasm and a willingness to ask questions. A company realizes a motivated person accepts added challenges and does that little bit extra on every job.

> *Communication Skills:* More than ever, the ability to talk and write effectively to people at all levels in a company is a key to success.

> *Chemistry:* The company representative is looking for someone who does not get rattled, wears a smile, is confident without self-importance, gets along with others; who is, in short, a team player.

> *Energy:* Someone who always gives that extra effort in the little things as well as important matters.

> *Determination:* Someone who does not back off when a problem or situation gets tough.

> *Confidence:* Not braggadocio. Poise. Friendly, honest, and open with all employees high or low. Neither intimidated by the big enchiladas, nor overly familiar.

Professional Profile:

All companies seek employees who respect their profession and employer. Projecting these professional traits will identify you as loyal, reliable, and trustworthy:

Reliability: Following up on yourself, not relying on anyone else to ensure the job is well done, and keeping management informed every step of the way.

Honesty/Integrity: Taking responsibility for your actions, both good and bad. Always making decisions in the best interests of the company, never on whim or personal preference.

Pride: Pride in a job well done. Always taking the extra step to make sure the job is done to the best of your ability. Paying attention to the details.

Dedication: Whatever it takes in time and effort to see a project through to completion, on deadline.

Analytical Skills: Weighing the pros and cons. Not jumping at the first solution to a problem that presents itself. The short- and long-term benefits of a solution against all its possible negatives.

Listening Skills: Listening and understanding, as opposed to waiting your turn to speak.

Achievement Profile:

Earlier, I discussed that companies have very limited interests: making money, saving money (the same as making money), and saving time, which does both. Projecting your achievement profile, in however humble a fashion, is the key to winning any job.

Money Saved: Every penny saved by your thought and efficiency is a penny earned for the company.

Time Saved: Every moment saved by your thought and efficiency enables your company to save money and make more in the additional time available. Double bonus.

Money Earned: Generating revenue is the goal of every company.

Projecting your business profile is important on those occasions when you cannot demonstrate ways you have made money, saved money, or saved time for previous employers. These keys demonstrate you are always on the lookout for opportunities to contribute, and that you keep your boss informed when an opportunity arises.

> *Efficiency:* Always keeping an eye open for wastage of time, effort, resources, and money.
>
> *Economy:* Most problems have two solutions: an expensive one, and one that the company would prefer to implement.
>
> *Procedures:* Procedures exist to keep the company profitable. Don't work around them. This also means keeping your boss informed. You tell your boss about problems or good ideas, not his or her boss. Follow the chain of command. Do not implement your own "improved" procedures or organize others to do so.
>
> *Profit:* The reason all the above traits are so universally admired in the business world is because they relate to profit.

□ □ □

As the requirements of the job are unfolded for you at the interview, meet them point by point with your qualifications. If your experience is limited, stress the key profile traits, your relevant interests, and desire to learn. If you are weak in just one particular area, keep your mouth shut; perhaps that dimension will not arise. If the area is probed, be prepared to handle and overcome the negative by stressing additional complementary skills that compensate.

Do not show discouragement if the interview appears to be going poorly. You have nothing to gain by showing defeat, and it could merely be an interview tactic to test your self-confidence.

If for any reason you get flustered or lost, keep a straight face and posture; gain time to marshal your thoughts by asking, "Could you help me with that?" or, "Would you run that by me again?" or, "That's a good question; I want to be sure I understand. Could you please explain that again?"

□ □ □

Now it is time for you to study the tough questions. Use the examples and explanations to build answers that promote your background and skills.

□ *"What are the reasons for your success in this profession?"*

With this question, the interviewer is not interested in examples of your success—he wants to know what makes you tick. Keep your answers short, general, and to the point. Using your work experience, personalize and use value keys from your personal profile, professional profile, and business profile. For example, "I attribute my success to three reasons: the support I've always received from co-workers, which always encourages me to be cooperative and look at my specific job in terms of what we as a department are trying to achieve. This gives me great pride in my work and its contribution to the department's efforts. Finally, I find that every job has its problems that need solutions, and while there's always a costly solution, there's usually an economical one as well, whether it's in terms of time or money."

□ *"What is your energy level like? Describe a typical day."*

You must demonstrate good use of your time, that you believe in planning your day beforehand, and that when it is over, you review your own performance to make sure you are reaching the desired goals. No one wants a part-time employee, so you should sell your energy level. For example, your answer might end with: "At the end of the day when I'm ready to quit, I make a rule always to type one more letter [make one more call, etc.], and clear my desk for the next day."

□ *"Why do you want to work here?"*

To answer this question, you must have researched the company and built a dossier. Your research work from Chapter One is now rewarded. You should reply with the company's attributes as you see them. Cap your answer with reference to your belief that this can provide you with a stable and happy work environment—the interviewer's company has that reputation—and that such an atmosphere would encourage your best work.

"I'm not looking for just another paycheck. I enjoy my work and am proud of my profession. Your company produces a superior product. I think that gives us certain things in common, and means I would fit in well with your team."

☑ *"What kind of experience do you have for this job?"*

This is a golden opportunity to sell yourself, but before you do, be sure you know what is most critical to the interviewer. The interviewer is not just looking for a competent engineer, typist, or salesperson; he or she is looking for someone who can contribute quickly to the current projects. When interviewing, companies invariably give everyone a broad picture of the job, but the person they hire will be a problem-solver, someone who can contribute to the specific projects in the first six months. Only by asking will you identify the areas of your interviewer's greatest urgency and therefore interest.

If you do not know the projects you will be involved with in the first six months, you must ask. Level-headedness and analytical ability are respected, and you will naturally answer the question more appropriately. For example, a company experiencing shipping problems might appreciate this answer: "My high-speed machining background and familiarity with your equipment will allow me to contribute quickly. I understand deadlines, delivery schedules, and the importance of getting the product shipped. Finally, my awareness of economy and profit has always kept reject parts to a bare minimum."

☐ *"Are you willing to go where the company sends you?"*

Unfortunately with this one you are, as the saying goes, "damned if you do and damned if you don't." What is the *real* question? Do they want you to relocate or just travel on business? If you simply answer "no," you will not get the job offer, but if you answer "yes," you could end up in Monkey's Eyebrow, Kentucky. So play for time and ask, "Are you talking about business travel, or is the company relocating?" In the final analysis, your answer should be "yes." You don't have to accept the job, but without the offer you have no decision to make. Your single goal at an interview is to sell yourself and win a job offer. Never forget, only when you have the offer is there a decision to make about that particular job.

☑ *"What did you like/dislike about your last job?"*

Most interviews start with a preamble by the interviewer about his company. Pay attention: this information will help you answer the question. In fact, any statement the interviewer makes about the job or corporation can be used to your advantage.

So in answer, you liked everything about your last job. You might even say your company taught you the importance of certain keys from the business profile, achievement profile, or professional profile. Criticizing a prior employer is a warning flag that you could be a problem employee. No one intentionally hires trouble, and that is what's behind the question. Keep your answers short and positive. You are only allowed one negative about past employers, and only then if your interviewer has a "hot button" about his department or company; if so, you will have written it down on your notepad, in which case the only thing your past employer could not offer was, for example: "The ability to contribute more in different areas in the smaller environment you have here. I really liked everything about the job. The reason I want to leave it is to find a position where I can make a greater contribution. You see, I work for a big company that is encouraging increasing specialization of skills. The smaller environment you have here will, as I said, allow me to contribute far more in different areas." Tell them what they want to hear; replay the hot button.

Of course, if you interview with a large company, turn it around. "I work for a small company and don't get the time to specialize in one or two major areas . . ." Then replay the hot button.

☑ *"How do you feel about your progress to date?"*

This question is not geared solely to rate your progress; it also rates your self-esteem (personal profile keys). Be positive, yet do not give the impression you have already done your best work. Make the interviewer believe you see each day as an opportunity to learn and contribute, and that you see the environment at this company as conducive to your best efforts.

"Given the parameters of my job, my progress has been excellent. I know the work and understand the importance of the role it plays within my company's operations. I feel I am just reaching that point in my career when I can make significant contributions."

☐ *"How long would you stay with the company?"*

The interviewer might be thinking of offering you a job. So you must encourage him or her to sell you on the job. With a tricky question like this, end your answer with a question of your own that really puts the ball back in the interviewer's court. Your reply might be: "I would really like to settle down with this company. I take direction well and love to learn. As long as I am growing professionally, there is no reason for me to make a move. How long do you think I would be happy here?"

☐ *"Have you done the best work you are capable of doing?"*

Say "yes," and the interviewer will think you're a has-been. As with all these questions, personalize your work history and include the essence of this reply: "I'm proud of my professional achievements to date, but I believe the best is yet to come. I am always motivated to give my best efforts, and in this job there are always opportunities to contribute when you stay alert."

☐ *"How long would it take you to make a contribution to our company?"*

Again, be sure to qualify the question: In what area does the interviewer need rapid contributions? You are best advised to answer this question with a question: "That is an excellent question. To help me answer, what do you anticipate my responsibilities will be for the first six or seven months?" You give yourself time to think while the interviewer concentrates on images of you working for the company. When your time comes to answer, start with: "Let's say I started on Monday the 17th. It will take me a few weeks to settle down and learn the ropes. I'll be earning my keep very quickly, but making a real contribution . . . *[hesitant pause]* . . . Do you have a special project in mind you will want me to get involved with?" This response could lead directly to a job offer, but if not, you already have the interviewer thinking of you as an employee.

☑ *"What would you like to be doing five years from now?"*

The safest answer contains a desire to be regarded as a true professional and team player. As far as promotion, that depends on finding a manager with whom you can grow. Of course, you will ask what opportunities exist within the company before being any more specific: "From what I know and what you have told me about the growth here, it seems operations is where the heavy emphasis is going to be. It seems that's where you need the effort and where I could contribute most toward the company's goals."

☑ *"What are your qualifications?"*

Again, you need to qualify the question. Does the interviewer want job-related or academic qualifications? Ask. If he or she is looking for job qualifications, you need to know exactly the work you'll be doing in the first few months. Again notice the importance of understanding the current projects and therefore the problems that need to be tackled. Ask. Then use appropriate value keys from all four categories tied in with relevant skills and achievements. You might say: "I can give you a general answer, but I feel my answer might be more valuable if you could tell me about specific work assignments in the early months . . ."

Or: "If the major task right now is reducing the reject ratio, I should tell you this. I work in a high-speed manufacturing environment, and since I've been there, I've reduced rejects 26 percent . . ."

☑ *"What are your biggest accomplishments?"*

Keep your answers job-related; from earlier exercises, a number of
achievements should spring to mind. If you exaggerate contributions
to major projects, you will be accused of suffering from "coffee machine
syndrome," the affliction of a junior clerk who claimed success for an
Apollo space mission based on his relationships with certain scientists,
established at the coffee machine. You might begin your reply with:
"Although I feel my biggest achievements are still ahead of me, I am
proud of my involvement with . . . I made my contribution as part of
that team and learned a lot in the process. We did it with hard work,
concentration, and an eye for the bottom line."

☑ *"Can you work under pressure?"*

You might be tempted to give a simple yes or no answer, but don't.
It reveals nothing and you lose the opportunity to sell your skills and
value profiles. Actually, this common question often comes from an
unskilled interviewer, because it is closed-ended. As such, it does not
give you the chance to elaborate. Whenever you are asked one of these,
mentally add: "Please give me a brief yet comprehensive answer."
Do this, and you will give the information requested and seize an
opportunity to sell yourself. For example, you could say: "Yes, I usually
find it stimulating. However, I believe in planning and proper management of my time to reduce panic deadlines within my area of responsibility."

☑ *"What is your greatest strength?"*

Key to your background and build in a couple of the key value profiles
from different categories. You will want to demonstrate pride, reliability, ability to stick with a difficult task yet change courses rapidly
when required. You can rearrange the previous answer here. Your
answer in part might be: "I believe in planning and proper management
of my time. And yet I can still work under pressure."

☑ *"What interests you most about this job?"*

Be straightforward, unless you haven't been given adequate information to determine an answer, in which case you should ask a question of your own to clarify. Perhaps you could say, "Before answering, could you tell me a little more about the role this job plays in the departmental goals?" or, "Where is the biggest vacuum in your department at the moment?" The additional information you gather with these questions provides the appropriate slant to your answer: that is, what is of greatest benefit to the department and to the company. Careerwise, this obviously has the greatest benefit to you, too. Your answer then displays the personality traits that support the existing need. Your answer in part might include, "I'm looking for a challenge and an opportunity to make a contribution, so if you feel the biggest challenge in the department is . . . I'm the one for the job." Then include the personality traits that support your statements. Perhaps: "I like a challenge, my background demonstrates excellent problem-solving abilities, and I always see a project through to the finish."

☐ *"How much money do you want?"*

This is a knock-out question; give the wrong answer, and you will immediately be eliminated. It is always a temptation to ask for the moon knowing you can come down, but that is a poor approach. Companies have strict salary ranges (called salary curves) for every job, so giving an ill-considered answer can reduce your job-offer chances to zero. The solution? You need the best offer possible without pricing yourself out of the market, so it's time to dance: "I naturally want to make as much as my background and experience permits. I was/am making X dollars. The most important thing to me, however, is the job and the people I will be working with. If I am right for the job, and I believe I am, I feel sure you'll make me a fair offer." You may tag a question onto the end of this response: "What figure did you have in mind?"

☐ *"What are you looking for in your next job?"*

You want a company where your personal profile keys and professional profile keys will allow you to contribute to business value keys. Avoid saying what you want the company to give you; you must say what you want in terms of what *you* can give to your employer. The key word in the following example is "contribution": "My experience at the XYZ Corporation has shown me I have a talent for motivating people. This is demonstrated by my team's absenteeism dropping 20 percent, turnover steadying at 10 percent, and production increasing 12 percent. I am looking for an opportunity to continue that kind of contribution, and a company and supervisor who will help me develop in a professional manner."

☑ *"Why should I hire you?"*

Your answer will be short and to the point. It will highlight areas from your background that relate to current needs and problems. Recap the interviewer's description of the job, meeting it point by point with your skills. Finish your answer with: "I have qualifications, I'm a team player, I take direction, and have the desire to make a thorough success."

☑ *"What can you do for us that someone else cannot do?"*

This question will come only after a full explanation of the job has been given. Recap the interviewer's job description, then follow with: "I can bring to this job a determination to see projects through to a proper conclusion. I listen and take direction well. I am analytical and don't jump to conclusions. And finally, I understand we are in business to make a profit, so I keep an eye on cost and return. How do these qualifications fit your needs?"

   You finish with a question that asks for feedback or a powerful answer. If you haven't covered the interviewer's hot buttons, he or she will cover them now, and you can respond accordingly.

☑ *"Describe a difficult problem you've had to deal with."*

This is a favorite tough question. It is designed to probe your professional profile; specifically, your analytical skills: "Well, I always follow a five-step format with a difficult problem. One, I stand back and examine the problem. Two, I recognize the problem as the symptom of other, perhaps hidden, factors. Three, I make a list of possible solutions to the problem. Four, I weigh both the consequences and cost of each solution, and determine the best solution. And five, I go to my boss, outline the problem, make my recommendation, and ask for my superior's advice and approval.''

Then give an example of a problem and your solution. For example: "When I joined my present company, I filled the shoes of a manager who had been fired. Turnover was very high. My job was to reduce the turnover, improve morale, and increase sales. Sales of our new copier had slumped for the fourth quarter in a row. The new employer was very concerned, and he even gave me permission to clean house. The cause of the problem? The sales team had never had any sales training. All my people needed was an intensive sales training course. My boss gave me permission to join the American Society of Training and Development, which cost $125. With what I learned there, I turned the department around. Sales continued to slump in my first quarter. Then they skyrocketed. Management was pleased with the sales, my boss was pleased because the solution was effective and cheap. I only had to replace two salespeople.''

☑ *"What have you learned from jobs you have held?''*

Tie your answer to your business and professional profile. The interviewer needs to understand that you seek and can accept constructive advice, and that your business decisions are based on the ultimate good of the company, not your personal whim or preference. "More than anything, I have learned that what is good for the company is good for me. So I listen very carefully to directions and always keep my boss informed of my actions.''

The profiles you have projected in this answer are:

● Listening Skills (professional profile)

● Your concern for the bottom line (business profile)

- Your willingness to follow procedures (business profile)

☐ *"What would your references say?"*

You have nothing to lose by being positive. If you demonstrate how well you and your boss got along, the interviewer does not have to ask, "What do you dislike about your current manager?"

The higher up the corporate ladder you climb, the more likely it is that references will be checked. It is a good idea to ask past employers to give you a letter of recommendation. This way you know what is being said. It reduces the chances of the company representative checking up on you, and if you are asked this question you can pull out a sheaf of rousing accolades and hand them over. If your references are checked by the company, they must *by law* have your written permission. This permission is usually included in the application form you sign.

☑ *"What type of decisions did you make on your last job?"*

Your answer should include reference to the fact that your decisions were all based on appropriate business profile keys. The interviewer may be searching to define your responsibilities or he or she may want to know that you don't overstep yourself. It is also an opportunity, however humble your position, to show your achievement profile.

For example: "Being in charge of the mailroom, my job is to make sure people get information in a timely manner. The job is well defined, and my decisions aren't that difficult. I noticed a year or two ago that when I took the mail around at 10 a.m., everything stopped for 20 minutes. I had an idea and gave it to my boss. She got it cleared by the president, and ever since, we take the mail around just before lunch. Mr. Gray, the president, thinks my idea improved productivity and saved time."

☐ *"Why were you fired?"*

This is a *very* difficult question to answer, because you have to overcome the stigma of being terminated. Looking at that painful event objectively, you will probably find the cause of your dismissal rooted in the absence of one or more of the 20 profiles. Having been fired also creates instant doubt in the mind of the interviewer, and greatly increases the chances of your references being checked. So you must bite the bullet and call the person who fired you, find out why it happened, and what they would say about you today.

Whatever you do, don't advertise the fact you were fired. If you are asked, be honest, but make sure you have packaged the reason in the best light possible. Perhaps: "I'm sorry to say, but I deserved it. I was having some personal problems at the time and I let it affect my work. I was late to work and lost my motivation. My supervisor—who, by the way, I still speak to—had directions to trim the workforce anyway, and as I was hired only a couple of years ago, I was *one* of the first to go."

If you can find out the employee turnover figures, voluntary or otherwise, you might add: "Fifteen other people have left so far this year." A combination answer of this nature minimizes the stigma. You have even managed to demonstrate that you take responsibility for your actions, which shows your analytical and listening skills. If one of your past managers will speak well of you, there is nothing to lose and everything to gain by finishing with: "Jill Johnson, at the company, would be a good person to check for a reference on what I have told you."

Of course being terminated for circumstances outside your control (plant shutdown, for example) is perfectly acceptable, and should be explained in a forthright manner.

☑ *"In your last job, what were some of the things you spent most of your time on, and why?"*

Employees come in two categories: goal-oriented (those who want to get the job done), and task-oriented (those who believe in "busy" work). You must demonstrate good time management, and that you are, therefore, goal-oriented, for that is what this question probes.

You might reply: "I work on the telephone like a lot of business-

people; meetings also take up a great deal of time. What is more important to me is effective time management. I find more gets achieved in
a shorter time if a meeting is scheduled, say, immediately before lunch
or at the close of business. I try to block my time in the morning and
afternoon for major tasks, so I don't get bogged down in 'busy' work.
At 4 o'clock, I review what I've achieved, what went right or wrong,
and plan adjustments and my main thrust of business for tomorrow.''

☑ *"In what ways has your job prepared you to take on greater responsibility?"*

This is one of the most important questions you will have to answer. The
interviewer is looking for examples of your professional growth, so you
must tell a story that demonstrates it. The following example shows
growth, listening skills, honesty, and adherence to procedures. Parts of
it can be adapted to your personal experience. Notice the "then and
now" aspect of the answer.

"In the early days my boss would brief me morning and evening. I
made some mistakes, learned a lot, and got the jobs in on time. Nowadays, I meet with her every Monday for breakfast to discuss any major
directional changes."

11.
Negatives and Tricks

These awful-sounding questions are thrown in to test your poise, to see how you react under pressure, and to plumb the depths of your confidence. Many people ruin their chances by reacting to these questions as personal insults rather than the challenge and opportunity to shine that they *really* represent.

These trick questions can be turned to your advantage or merely avoided by your nifty footwork. Whichever, you will be among a select few who understand this line of questioning.

Remember with these questions to build a personalized answer that reflects your experience and profession. Practice them aloud: by doing this, your responses to these interview gambits will become part of you. This enhancement of your mental attitude will positively affect your confidence during an interview.

Especially in this chapter, reflexive questions will be very useful. Negative or trick questions are designed to sort out the clutch players from those who wilt under pressure. Used with discretion, the reflexives will prove to the interviewer that you are able to function under pressure, and you put the ball back in the interviewer's court.

□

☐ *"I'm not sure you're suitable for the job."*

The interviewer's "I'm not sure" *really* means, "I'd like to hire you, so here's a wide open opportunity to sell me." He or she is probing three areas from your personal profile: your confidence, determination, and listening profiles. Remain calm mentally and physically. Put the ball straight back into the interviewer's court: "Why do you say that?" You need both the information and time to think up an appropriate reply, but it is important to show that you are not intimidated. Work out a program of action for this question; even if the interviewer's point regarding your skills is valid, come back with value keys and alternate compatible skills. You counter with other skills that show your competence and learning ability, and use them to show you can pick up the new skills quickly. Tie the two together and demonstrate that with your other attributes you can bring many pluses to the job. Finish your answer with a reflexive question that encourages a "yes" answer.

"I admit my programming skills in that language are a little light. However, all programming languages have similarities. My experience demonstrates that with a competence in four other languages, getting up to speed with this one will take only a short while, plus I can bring a depth of other experience to the job, wouldn't you agree?"

If the reason for the question is not a lack of technical skills, it must be a question about one of your key profile areas. Perhaps the interviewer will say, "You haven't convinced me of your determination." This is an invitation to sell yourself, so tell a story that demonstrates determination.

For example: "It's interesting you should say that. My present boss is convinced of my determination. About a year ago we were having some problems with a union organization in the plant. Management's problem was our 50 percent Spanish monolingual production workforce. Despite the fact that our people had the best working conditions and benefits in the area, they were strongly pro-union. If successful, we would be the first unionized division in the company. No one in management spoke Spanish. I took a crash Berlitz course, two hours at home every night for five weeks. Then I got one of the maintenance crew to help me with my grammar and diction. Then a number of other production workers started saying simple things to me in Spanish and helping me with the answers. I opened the first meeting with the workforce to discuss the problems. My 'Buenos dias. Me llamo Brandon,' got a few cheers. We had demonstrated that we cared enough to try to communicate. Our division never did unionize, and my determination to take the extra step paid off and allowed my superiors to negotiate from a position of caring and strength. Wouldn't you agree that shows determination?''

☑ *"What is your greatest weakness?"*

This is a direct invitation to put your head in a noose. Decline the invitation. Your best chance is to give a generalized answer that takes advantage of value keys. Design the answer so that your "weakness" is ultimately a positive characteristic. For example: "I enjoy my work and always give each project my best shot. So when sometimes I don't feel others are pulling their weight, I find it a little frustrating. I am aware of this weakness, and in these situations I try to overcome it with a positive attitude that I hope will catch on."

Congratulations, you have just turned a bear of a question into an opportunity to sell yourself with your professional profile.

☐ *"Wouldn't you feel better off in another company?"*

Answer "no" and explain why. All the interviewer wants to see is how much you know about the company and how determined you are to join its ranks. Your earlier research and knowledge of personal profile keys (determination) will pay off again. Overcome the objection with an example, and show how this will help you contribute to the company; end with a question of your own. In this instance, the question has a twofold purpose: one, to identify a critical area to sell yourself; and two, to encourage the interviewer to consider an image of you working at the company.

You could reply: "Not at all. My whole experience has been with small companies. I am good at my job and in time could become a big fish in a little pond. But that is not what I want. This corporation is a leader in its business. You have a strong reputation for encouraging skills development in your employees. This is the type of environment

I want to work in. Now, coming from a small company, I have done a little bit of everything. That means that no matter what you throw at me, I will learn it quickly. For example, what would be the first project I would be involved with?''

☑ *"What kind of decisions are most difficult for you?"*

You are human, admit it, but be careful what you admit. If you have ever had to fire someone, you are in luck, because no one likes to do that. Emphasize that having reached a logical conclusion, you act. If you are not in management, tie your answer to key profiles: "It's not that I have difficulty making decisions, yet some require more consideration than others. A small example might be vacation time. Now, everyone is entitled to it, but I don't believe you should leave your boss in a bind at short notice. I think very carefully at the beginning of the year when I'd like to take my vacation, and then think of alternate dates. I go to my supervisor, tell him what I hope to do, and see whether there is any conflict. I wouldn't want to be out of the office for the two weeks prior to a project deadline, for instance. So by carefully considering things far enough in advance, I don't procrastinate, and I make sure my plans jibe with my boss and the department for the year.''

Here you take a trick question and use it to demonstrate your consideration, analytical abilities, concern for the department, and for the company bottom line.

☐ *"Why were you out of work for so long?"*

You must have a sound explanation for any and all gaps in your employment history. If not, you are unlikely to receive a job offer. Tell the truth; everyone understands it. Emphasize that you were not just looking for another paycheck. You are looking for a company to settle with and make a long-term contribution to.

"Well, I made a decision that I enjoy my work too much just to accept another paycheck. So I determined that the next job I took would be one where I could settle down and do my best to make a solid contribution. From everything I have heard about this company, you are a group that expects everybody to pull their weight, because you've got a real job to do. I like that, and I would like to be part of the team. What have I got to do to get the job?''

Answer the question. Compliment the interviewer and move the emphasis: from you being unemployed to how you can get the job offer.

☐ *"Why aren't your earning more at your age?"*

Accept this as a compliment to your skills and accomplishments. "I have always felt that solid experience would stand me in good stead in the long run and that earnings would come in due course. Also, I am not the type of person to change jobs just for the money. At this point, I have a solid background that is worth something to a company." Now, to avoid the interviewer putting you on the spot again, finish with a question: "How much *should* I be earning now?" The figure could be your offer.

☐ *'Why have you changed jobs so frequently?''*

If you have jumped around, blame it on youth (even the interviewer was young once). Now you realize what a mistake your job hopping was, and with your added domestic responsibilities you are now much more settled. Or you may wish to impress on the interviewer that your job-jumping was never as a result of poor performance, and that you grew professionally as a result of each job change.

You could reply: "My first job was a very long commute. I soon realized that, but I knew it would give me good experience in a very competitive field. Subsequently, I found a job much closer to home where the commute was only an hour each way. I was very happy at my second job. However, I got an opportunity to really broaden my experience base with a new company that was starting up. With the wisdom of hindsight, I realize that was a mistake; it took me six months to realize I couldn't make a contribution there. I've been with my current company a reasonable length of time. So I have broad experience in different environments. I didn't *just* job hop. So you see, I have more experience than the average person of my years. Now I want to settle down and make all my diverse background pay off in my contributions to my new employer. I certainly have an idea of what the competition is up to, wouldn't you agree?''

☑ *"Why do you want to leave your current job?"* or, *"Why did you leave your last job?"*

This is a common trick question. You *should* have an acceptable reason for leaving every job you have held, but if you don't, pick one of the six acceptable reasons from the employment industry formula, CLAMPS:

- C for *challenge.* You weren't able to grow professionally in that position.

- L for *location.* The commute was unreasonably long.

- A for *advancement.* There was nowhere for you to go. You had the talent, but there were too many people ahead of you.

- M for *money.* You were underpaid for your skills and contribution.

- P for *pride* or *prestige.* You wanted to be with a better company.

- S for *security.* The company was not stable.

"My last company was a family-owned affair. I had gone as far as I was able. It just seemed time for me to join a more prestigious company and accept greater challenges."

☑ *"What interests you least about this job?"*

This question is potentially explosive, but easily defused. Regardless of your occupation, there is at least one repetitive, mindless duty that everyone groans about and which goes with the territory. Use that as your example in a statement of this nature: "Filing is probably the least demanding part of the job. However, it is important to the overall success of my department, so I try to do it with a smile." You understand that it is necessary to take the rough with the smooth in any job.

☑ *"What was there about your last company that you didn't particularly like or agree with?"*

You are being checked out as a potential fly in the ointment. If you *have* to answer, it might be the way the company policies and/or directives were sometimes consciously misunderstood by some employees who disregard the bottom-line profitability of the corporation.

Or: "You know how it is sometimes with a big company. People lose awareness of the cost of things. There never seemed to be much concern about economy or efficiency. Everyone wanted his or her year-end bonus, but only worried about it in December. The rest of the year, nobody gave a hoot. I think that's the kind of thing we could be aware of most every day, don't you agree?"

☐ *"What do you feel is a satisfactory attendance record?"*

There are two answers to this question: one if you are in management, one if you are not. As a manager: "I believe attendance is a matter of management, motivation, and psychology. Letting the employees know you expect their best efforts and won't accept half-baked excuses is one thing. The other is to keep your employees motivated by a congenial work environment and the challenge of stretching themselves. Giving people pride in their work has a lot to do with it, too."

If you are not in management, the answer is even easier: "I've never really considered it; I work for a living, I enjoy my job, and I'm rarely sick."

☐ *"What is your general impression of your last company?"*

Always answer "very good." Keep your real feelings to yourself, whatever they might be. There is a strong belief among the American management fraternity that people who complain about past employers will cause problems for their new ones. Your answer is "very good" or "excellent." Then shut up.

☑ *"What are some of the problems you encounter in doing your job, and what do you do about them?"*

Note well the old saying, "A poor workman blames his tools." Your awareness that careless mistakes cost the company good money means you are always on the lookout for potential problems. Give an example of a problem you recognized and solved.

For example: "My job is fairly repetitive, so it's easy to overlook problems. Lots of people do. However, I always look for them; it helps keep me alert and motivated, so I do a better job. To give you an example, we make computer memory disks. Each one has to be machined by hand, and once completed, the slightest abrasion will turn one into a reject. I have a steady staff and little turnover, and everyone wears cotton gloves to handle the disks. Yet about six months ago, the reject rate suddenly went through the roof. Is that the kind of problem you mean? Well, the cause was one that could have gone unnoticed for ages. Jill, the section head who inspects all the disks, had lost a lot of weight, her diamond wedding band slipped around her finger, and it was scratching the disks as she passed them and stacked them to be shipped. Our main client was giving us a big problem over it, so my looking for problems and paying attention to detail really paid off."

The interviewer was trying to get you to reveal weak points; you avoided this trap.

☑ *"What are some of the things you find difficult to do? Why do you feel this way?"*

This is a variation on a couple of earlier questions. Remember, anything that goes against the best interests of your employer is difficult to do. If you are pressed for a job function you find difficult, answer in the past tense; that way, you show that you recognize the difficulty, but that you obviously handle it well.

"That's a tough question. There are so many things that are difficult to learn in our business, if you want to do the job right. I used to
have 40 clients to sell to every month, and I was so busy touching bases
with all of them, I never got a chance to sell to any of them. So I graded
them into three groups: the top 20 percent whom I did business with, I
called on every three weeks. The next group were those I sold to occasionally; these I called on once a month, but with a difference. Each
month, I marked 10 of them to spend time with and really get to know. I
still have difficulty reaching all 40 of my clients in a month, but my sales
have tripled, and are still climbing."

☑ *"Jobs have pluses and minuses. What were some of the minuses on
your last job?"*

A variation on the question, "What interests you least about this job?"
which was handled earlier. Use the same type of answer. For example,
"Like any salesperson, I enjoy selling, not doing the paperwork. But
as I cannot expect the customer to get the goods, and me my commission, I grin and bear it. Besides, if I don't do the paperwork, that holds
up other people in the company."

If you are not in sales, use the salesforce as a scapegoat. "In accounts
receivable, it's my job to get the money in to make payroll and good
things like that. Half the time, the goods get shipped before I get the
paperwork because sales says, 'It's a rush order.' That's a real minus
to me. It was so bad at my last company, we tried a new approach. We
met with sales and explained our problem. The result was that incre-
mental commissions were based on cash in, not on bill date. They saw
the connection, and things are much better now."

☑ *"What kind of people do you like to work with?"*

This is the easy part of a tricky three-part question. Obviously: people
who have pride, honesty, integrity, and dedication to their work. Now ..

☐ *"What kind of people do you find it difficult to work with?"*

The second part of the same question. You could say: "People who don't follow procedures, or slackers. The occasional rotten apples who don't really care about the quality of their work. They're long on complaints, but short on solutions." And the third part of the question . . .

☑ *"How have you successfully worked with this difficult type of person?"*

This is the most difficult part of the three-part question. To this you might reply: "I stick to my guns, keep enthusiastic, and hope some of it will rub off. I had a big problem with one guy; all he did was complain— and always in my area. Eventually, I told him how I felt. I said if I were a millionaire, I'd have all the answers and wouldn't have to work, but as it was, I wasn't, and had to work for a living. I told George that I really enjoyed his company, but I didn't want to hear it any more. Every time I saw him after that, I presented him with a work problem and asked his advice."

You can go on that sometimes you've noticed that such people simply lack enthusiasm and confidence, and that energetic and cheerful co-workers can often change this. "It got him involved with something constructive, instead of just moaning."

☐ *"How did you get your last job?"*

The interviewer is looking for initiative. If you can, show it. At the least, show determination.

"I was actually turned down for my last job as having too little experience. I asked the manager to give me a trial before he offered it to anyone else. I went in and asked for a list of companies they'd never sold to, picked up the phone, and in that hour I arranged two appointments. How did I get the job? In a word, determination!"

☐ ☐ ☐

If you are asked and successfully handle these trick and negatively-phrased questions, the interviewer will be looking at you favorably. You may well expect next a series of questions that will tell the interviewer how you will behave once on the job: "What kind of person are you *really*, Mr. Jones?"

12.
"What Kind of Person Are You *Really,* Mr. Jones?"

Will you reduce your new employer's life expectancy? The interviewer wants to know! If you are offered the job and accept, you will be working together 50 weeks of the year. Every employer wants to know whether you will fit in with the rest of the staff, whether you are a team player, and most of all: Are you manageable?

There are a number of questions the interviewer might use to probe this area. They will mainly be geared to your behavior and attitudes in the past. Remember: it is universally believed that your past actions predict your future behavior.

☑ *"How do you take direction?"*

This is really two questions. "How do you take direction?" and, "How do you take criticism?" Your answer will cover both points. "I take direction well and believe there are two types: carefully explained direction, when my boss has time to treat me with honor and respect; then there is the other—a brusque order or correction. While most people get upset with this, personally I always believe the manager is troubled with bigger problems and a tight schedule. As such I take the direction and get on with the job without taking offense so my boss can get on with her job. It's the only way.''

☐ *"Would you like to have your boss' job?"*

It is a rare boss who wants his or her livelihood taken. On my very first interview, my future boss said, "Mr. Yate, it has been a pleasure to meet you. However, until you walked in I wasn't looking for a new job. Don't you feel you would be better off with another company?"

By the same token, ambition is admired, but mainly by the ambitious. Be cautiously optimistic. Perhaps: "Well, if my boss were promoted over the coming years, I hope to have made a strong enough contribution to warrant his recommendation. And I realize there are more skills I have to learn. That's why I'm looking for a fresh opportunity. I'm looking for a manager who will help me develop my capabilities and grow with him."

☑ *"What do you think of your current/last boss?"*

Short, sweet, and shut up. People who complain about their employers are recognized to be the same people who cause the most disruption in the department. Being asked this question means the interviewer has no desire to hire trouble. "I liked her as a person, respected her professionally, and appreciated her guidance." This question is often followed by one that tries to validate your answer.

☑ *"Describe a situation where your work or an idea was criticized."*

A doubly dangerous question. You are being asked to say how you handle criticism and to detail your faults. If you are asked this question, describe a poor *idea* that was criticized, *not* poor work. Poor work can cost money and is a warning sign, obviously, to the interviewer.

One of the wonderful things about a new job is that you can leave the past entirely behind, so it does not matter how you handled criticism in the past. What does matter is how the interviewer would *like* you to handle criticism, if and when it becomes his or her unpleasant duty to dish it out; that's what the question is really about. So relate one of those "it-seemed-like-a-good-idea-at-the-time" ideas, and finish with how you handled the criticism. You could say: "I listened carefully and resisted the temptation to interrupt or defend myself. Then I fed back what I heard to make sure the facts were straight. I asked for advice, we bounced some ideas around, then I came back later and represented the idea in a more viable format. My supervisor's input was invaluable."

☑ *"Tell me about yourself."*

This is not an invitation to ramble on. You need to know more about the question before giving an answer. "What area of my background would be most interesting to you?" This will help the interviewer help you with the appropriate focus, so you can avoid discussing irrelevancies. Never answer this question without qualifying whether the interviewer wishes to hear about your business or personal life. However the interviewer responds to your qualifying question, the tale you tell should demonstrate one or more of the 20 key personality profiles. Perhaps honesty, integrity, being a team player, or determination. If you choose "team player," part of your answer might include this: "I put my heart into everything I do, whether it be sports or work. I find that getting along with your peers and being part of the team makes life more enjoyable and productive."

☐ *"What have you done that shows initiative?"*

The question probes whether you are a "doer," someone who will look for ways to increase sales, save time, or save money. The kind of person who gives a manager a pleasant surprise once in awhile, who makes life easier for coworkers. Do beware, however, that your example of initiative does not show a disregard for company policies and procedures.

"My boss has to organize a lot of meetings. That means developing agendas, letting employees around the country know the dates well in advance, getting materials printed, et cetera. Most people in my position sit and wait for the work to be given them. I don't. Every quarter I sit down with my boss and find out the dates of all his meetings for the next six months. I immediately make the hotel and flight arrangements and then work backwards. I ask myself questions like, 'If the agenda for the July meeting is to reach the field at least six weeks before the meeting, when must it be finished by?' Then I come up with a deadline. I do this for all the major activities for all the meetings. I put the deadlines in his diary; and mine, only two weeks earlier. That way I remind the boss that the deadline is getting close. My boss is the best organized, most relaxed manager in the company. None of his colleagues can understand how he does it."

☑ *"What are some of the things about which you and your supervisor disagreed?"*

It is safest to state that you did not disagree.

☑ *"In what areas do you feel your supervisor could have done a better job?"*

The same goes for this one. No one admires a Monday-morning quarterback

You could reply: "I have always had the highest respect for my supervisor. I have always been so busy learning from Mr. Jones that I don't think he could have done a better job. He has really brought me to the point where I am ready for greater challenges. That's why I'm here."

☑ *"What are some of the things your supervisor did that you disliked?"*

If you and the interviewer are both non-smokers, for example, and your boss isn't, use it. Apart from that: "You know, I've never thought of our relationship in terms of like or dislike. I've always thought our role was to get along together and get the job done."

☑ *"How well do you feel your boss rated your job performance?"*

This is one very sound reason to ask for written evaluations of your work before leaving a company. Instead of answering, you whip out the citations.

Many performance review procedures include an evaluation of your ability to accept greater challenge; perhaps yours do. If you *don't* have written references, perhaps: "My supervisor always rated my job performance well. In fact, I was always rated as being capable of accepting further responsibilities. The problem was there was nothing available in the company, that's why I'm here."

☐ *"How interested are you in sports?"*

A recently completed survey of middle- and upper-management personnel found that the executives who listed group sports/activities among their extracurricular activities made an average of $3,000 per year *more* than their sedentary colleagues. Don't you just love baseball, suddenly? The interviewer is looking for your involvement in groups, as a signal that you know how to get along with others and pull together as a team.

"I really enjoy most team sports. Don't get a lot of time to indulge myself, but I am a regular member of my company's softball team." Apart from team sports, endurance sports are seen as a sign of determination: swimming, running, and cycling are all okay.

☑ *"What personal characteristics are necessary for success in your field?"*

You know the answer to this one: it's a brief recital of key personality profiles.

You might say: "To be successful in my field? Drive, motivation, energy, confidence, determination, good communication, and analytical skills. Combined, of course, with the ability to work with others."

☑ *"Do you prefer working with others or alone?"*

This question is usually used to determine whether you are a team player. However, before answering be sure you know whether the job *requires* you to work alone. Then answer appropriately. Perhaps: "I'm quite happy working alone when necessary. I don't need much constant reassurance. But, I prefer to work in a group. So much more gets achieved when people pull together."

☐ *"Tell me a story."*

Wow. What on earth does the interviewer mean by that question? You don't know until you get him or her to elaborate. Ask, "What would you like me to tell you a story about?" Any other response is to risk making a fool of yourself. Very often the question is asked to see how analytical you are: people who answer the question without qualifying show that they do not think things through carefully. The subsequent question will be about either your personal or professional life. If it is about your personal life, tell a story that shows you like people and are determined. Do *not* discuss your love life. If the subsequent question is about your professional life, it might be:

☐ *"What have your other jobs taught you?"*

By all means, talk about the skills you have learned. Many interviewees have had success finishing their answer with: "There are two general things I have learned from past jobs. The first is: if you are confused, ask. It's better to ask a dumb question than make a stupid mistake. The second is: it is better to promise less and produce more."

☐ *"Define cooperation."*

The question asks you to explain how to function as a team player in the workplace. Your answer could be: "Cooperation is a person's ability to sacrifice personal wishes and beliefs whenever necessary to assure the department reaches its goals. It is also a person's desire to be part of a team, and by hard work and goodwill make the department greater than the sum of its parts."

☐ *"What difficulties do you have tolerating people with different backgrounds and interests from yours?"*

Another "team player" question with the awkward inference that you *do* have problems. Give the following answer: *"I don't have any."*

☐ ☐ ☐

Now if you think the interview is only tough for the interviewee, it's time to take a look at the other side of the desk.

13.
The Other Side
of the Desk

There are two terrible places to be during an interview: sitting in front of the desk wondering what on earth is going to happen next, and sitting behind the desk asking the questions. The average interviewer dreads the meeting almost as much as the interviewee, yet for opposite reasons.

American business frequently yields to the mistaken belief that any person, on being promoted into the ranks of management, becomes mystically endowed with all necessary managerial skills. This is a fallacy. Comparatively few management people have been taught to interview; most just bumble along and pick up a certain proficiency over a period of time.

There are two distinct types of interviewers who can spell disaster for you if you are unprepared. One is the highly skilled interviewer who has been trained in systematic techniques for probing your past for all the facts and evaluating your potential. The other is the totally incompetent interviewer who may even lack the ability to phrase a question adequately.

□ □ □

Skillful interviewers know exactly what they want to discover. They have taken exhaustive steps to learn the strategies that will help them hire only the best for their company. They follow a set format for the interview process to ensure objectivity in selection and a set sequence of questions to ensure the facts are gathered. This type of interviewer will definitely test your mettle.

There are many ways for a manager to build and conduct a structured interview, but all have the same goals:

- To ensure a systematic coverage of your work history and applicable job-related skills

- To provide a technique for gathering all the relevant facts

- To provide a uniform strategy that objectively evaluates all job candidates.

Someone using structured interview techniques will usually follow a standard format. The interview will begin with small talk and a brief introduction to relax you. Following close on the heels of this chit-chat comes a statement geared to assure you that baring your faults is the best way to get the job. Your interviewer will then outline the steps in the interview. This will include your giving a chronological description of your work history, and then the interviewer asking some questions about your experience. Then, prior to the close of the interview, you will be given an opportunity to ask your own questions.

Sounds pretty simple, huh? Well, watch out! The skilled interviewer knows exactly what questions will be asked, why they will be asked, in what order they will be asked, and what the desired responses are. Every applicant for the job will be interviewed and evaluated in exactly the same fashion. You are up against a pro.

Like the hunter who learns to think like his prey, the best way to win over this interviewer is to *think* like the interviewer. In fact, take the process a little further in subtlety: you must win, but you don't want the other guys to realize you beat them at their own game. To do this, you must learn how the interviewer has prepared for you; and by going through the same process you will beat out your competitors for the job offer.

The dangerous part of this type of interview is called "Skills Evaluation." The interviewer has analyzed all the different skills it takes to do the job, and all the personality traits that complement those skills. Armed with this data, he or she has developed a series of carefully-sequenced questions to draw out your relative merits and weaknesses.

Graphically, it looks like this:

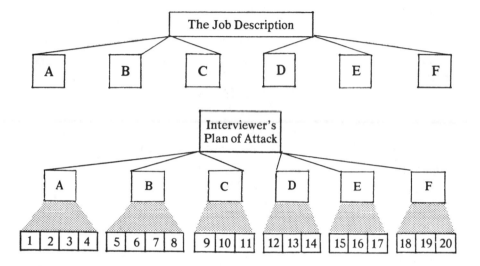

Letters A-F are the separate skills necessary to do the job; numbers 1-20 are questions asked to identify and verify that particular skill.

This is where many of the tough questions will arise. The only way to prepare effectively is to take the interviewer's viewpoint and complete this exercise in its entirety:

- Look at the position you seek: What role does it play in helping the company achieve its corporate mission and make a profit?

- What are the five most important duties of that job?

- From a management viewpoint, what are the skills and attributes necessary to perform each of these tasks?

Write all this down. This exercise requires a degree of objectivity, but it will generate multiple job offers.

Now, put yourself in the interviewer's shoes. What topics would you examine to find out whether a person can really do the job? If for some reason you get stuck in this process, just use your past experience. You have worked with good and bad people. Their work habits and skills will lead you to develop both the potential questions and the correct answers.

Each job skill you identify is fertile ground for the interviewer's questions. Don't forget the intangible skills that are so important to many jobs, like self-confidence or creativity, because the interviewer won't. Develop a number of questions for each job skill you identify.

Again looking back at coworkers (and still wearing the manager's mask), what are the personal characteristics that would make life comfortable or uncomfortable for you as a manager? These are also dimensions that are likely to be probed by the interviewer. Once you have identified the questions you would ask in the manager's position, the answers should come easily.

This is the way managers are trained to develop structured interview questions; I just gave you the inside track. Complete the exercise by developing the answers you would like to hear as a manager. Take time to complete the exercise conscientiously, writing out both the questions and appropriate answers.

□ □ □

These sharks have some juicy questions to probe your skills, attitude, and personality. Would you like to hear some of them? Notice that all the questions in this section lay out a problem, but in no way lead you to the answer. They are all two-part questions, and some are three. The additional question that can be tagged onto them *all* is, "What did you learn from this experience?" Assume this is included whenever you get one of these questions; you'll be able to sell different aspects of your success profile.

□

☑ *"You have been given a project that requires you to interact with different levels within the company. How do you do this? What levels are you most comfortable with?"*

This is a two-part question that probes your self-confidence. The first part asks how you interact with superiors and how you motivate those working for you on the project. The second part of the question is saying, "Tell me whom you regard as your peer group; help me to pigeonhole and categorize you." To cover these bases you will want to include the essence of this: "There are basically two types of people I would interact with on a project of this nature. Those I report to, who bear ultimate responsibility for its success. With them I determine deadlines and how they will evaluate the success of the project. I outline my approach, breaking the project down into component parts, getting approval on both the approach and costs. I would keep my supervisors up-to-date on a regular basis, and seek input whenever needed. My supervisors would expect three things from me: the facts, an analysis of potential problems, and that I not be intimidated, as this could jeopardize the project's success. I would comfortably satisfy all these expectations.

"The other people to interact with in a project like this are those who work with me and for me. With these people I would outline the project and explain how successful completion will benefit the company. I would assign the component parts to those best suited to each, arrange follow-up times to assure completion by deadline. My role here would be to direct, motivate, and bring the different personalities together to form a team.

"As to comfort level, I find this type of approach enables me to interact comfortably with all levels and types of people."

☑ *"Tell me about an event that really challenged you. How did you meet the challenge? In what way was your approach different from the others?"*

This is a straightforward two-part question. The first part probes your problem-solving abilities. The second asks you to set yourself apart from the herd. First of all, outline the problem. The blacker you make the situation look, the better. Having done this, go ahead and explain your solution, its value to your employer, and how it was different from other approaches.

"My company is a sales organization; I was responsible for 70 sales offices across the country. My job was to visit each office once a year, build market strategies with management, and train and motivate the sales force. Then the recession hit. The need to service the sales force was still there, but we couldn't justify the travel cost.

"Morale was an especially important factor; you can't let the sales force feel defeated. I reapportioned my reduced budget and did the following: I dramatically increased my telephone contact with the offices. I instituted a monthly sales technique letter—how to prospect for new clients, how to negotiate difficult sales, et cetera. I bought and rented sales training and motivational tapes and sent them to my managers with instructions on how to use them in a sales meeting. I stopped visiting all the offices. Instead, I scheduled weekend training meetings in central locations throughout my area: one day of sales training and one day of management training—how to run sales meetings, early termination of low producers, et cetera.

"While my colleagues complained about the drop in sales, mine increased, albeit a modest six percent. After two quarters my approach was officially adopted by the company."

☑ *"Give me an example of a method of working you have used. How did you feel about it?"*

You have a choice of giving an example of either good or bad work habits. Give a good example; one that demonstrates your understanding of corporate goals, your organization skills, analytical ability, or time management skills.

You could say: "I believe in giving an honest day's work for a day's pay. That requires organization and time management. I do my paperwork at the end of each day, when I review the day's achievements; with this done, I plan for tomorrow. When I come to work in the morning, I'm ready to get going without wasting time. I try to schedule meetings right before lunch; people get to the point more quickly if it's on their time. I feel this is a most efficient and organized method of working."

☐ *"When you joined your last company and met the group for the first time, how did you feel? How did you get on with them?"*

Your answer should include, "I naturally felt a little nervous, but I was excited about the new job. I shared that excitement with my new friends, told them that I was enthusiastic about learning new skills from them. I was open and friendly, and when given the opportunity to help someone myself, I jumped at it."

☐ *"In your last job, how did you plan to interview?"*

That's an easy one. Just give a description of how the skilled interviewer prepares.

☑ *"What would you do when you had a decision to make and no procedure existed?"*

This question probes your analytical skills, integrity, and dedication. Most of all, the interviewer is testing your reaction to the "company way of doing things." You need to cover that with: "I would only act without supervisor's direction if the situation was urgent and the supervisor was not available. Then, I would take command of the situation, make a decision, and implement it. I would update my boss at the earliest opportunity." If possible, tell a story to illustrate.

There are two questions that every skilled interviewer will use, especially if you are giving good answers. They will look for "negative balance." It will happen like this:

☑ *"Miss Jones, that is an excellent answer. Now to give me a balanced view, can you give me an example that didn't work out so well?"*

With this question you are required to give an example of an inadequacy. The trick is to pull something from the past, not the present, and to finish with what you learned from the experience. For example: "That's easy. When I first joined the workforce, I didn't really understand the importance of systems and procedures. There was one time when I was too anxious to contribute and didn't have the full picture. There was a sales visit report everyone had to fill out after visiting a customer. I always put a lot of effort into it until I realized it was never read; just went in the files. So I stopped doing it for a few days to see if it made any difference. I thought I was gaining time to make more sales for the company. I was so proud of my extra sales calls I told the boss at the end of the week. My boss explained that the records were for the long term, so that should my job change, the next salesperson would have the benefit of a full client history. It was a long time ago, but I have *never* forgotten the lesson: there's always a reason for systems and procedures. I've had the best-kept records in the company ever since."

Then the skilled interviewer will look for "negative confirmation" by saying, "Thank you, now can you give me another example?" The interviewer is trying to confirm a weakness. If you help, you could well do yourself out of a job. Your reaction is this: you sit deep in thought for a good 10 seconds, then look up and say *firmly:* "No, that's the only occasion when anything like that happened." Shut up and refuse to be further enticed.

□ □ □

Now you should be ready for almost anything a professional interviewer could throw at you. Your foresight and strategic planning will generate multiple offers of employment for you in all circumstances except one, and that's when you face the unconsciously incompetent interviewer. This one circumstance is probably more dangerous to your job-offer status than everything else combined.

This problem is embodied in the experienced manager who is a poor interviewer, but who does not know it. This person, consciously or otherwise, bases hiring decisions on "experience" and "knowledge of mankind" and "gut feeling." He or she is an Unconscious Incompetent. You have probably been interviewed by one in your time. Remember leaving an interview and, upon reflection, feeling the interviewer knew absolutely nothing about you or your skills? If so, you know how frustrating that can be. Here, you'll see how to turn this difficult situation to your advantage. In the future, good managers who are poor interviewers will be offering you jobs with far greater frequency than ever before. Understand that a poor interviewer can be a wonderful manager; interviewing skills are learned, not inherited or created as a result of a mystical corporate blessing.

The Unconscious Incompetents abound. Their heinous crime can only be exceeded by your inability *to recognize and take advantage of* the proffered opportunity.

As in handling the Skilled Interviewer, it is necessary to imagine how the Unconscious Incompetent thinks and feels.

There are many manifestations of the poor interviewer. After each example, follow instructions for appropriate handling of the unique problems each type poses for you.

☐ *Example One:* The interviewer's desk is cluttered, and the resume or application that was handed to him or her a few minutes before cannot be found.

Response: Sit quietly through the bumbling and search. Check out the surroundings. Breathe deeply and slowly to calm any natural interview nerves. As you bring your adrenalin under control, you do the same thing to the interviewer and the interview. This first example is usually the most common sign of the Unconscious Incompetent.

☐ *Example Two:* The interviewer experiences constant interruptions from the telephone or people walking into the office.

Response: This provides good opportunities for selling yourself. Make note on your pad of where you were in the conversation and refresh the interviewer on the point when you start talking again. He or she will be impressed with your level head and good memory. These interruptions also give time, perhaps, to find something of common interest in the office, something you can compliment. You will also have time to compose the suitable Value Key follow-up to the point made in the conversation prior to the interruption.

☐ *Example Three:* This is the interviewer who starts with an explanation of why you are both sitting there, and then allows the conversation to degenerate into a lengthy diatribe about the company.

Response: Show interest in the company and the conversation. Sit straight, look attentive (the other applicants probably fall asleep), make appreciative murmurs, and nod at the appropriate times until there is a pause. When this occurs, comment that this background of the company is much appreciated, because you can now see more clearly how the job fits into the general scheme of things; that you see, for example, how valuable communication skills would be for the job. Could the interviewer please tell you some of the other job requirements? Then, as the job's functions are described, you can interject appropriate information about your background with: "Would it be of value, Mr. Smith, if I described my experience with . . . ?"

☐ *Example Four:* In this example, the interviewer begins with, or quickly breaks into, the drawbacks of the job. The job may even be described in totally negative terms. This is often done without giving a balanced view of the duties and expectations of the position.

Response: An initial negative description invariably means the interviewer has had bad experiences hiring for this position. Your course is to *empathize* (not sympathize) with his bad experiences and make it known that you recognize the importance of (for example) *reliability,* especially in this particular type of job. (You will invariably find in these instances that what your interviewer has lacked in the past is someone with a serious understanding of Value Keys.) Illustrate your proficiency in this particular aspect of your profession with a short example from your work history. Finish your statements by asking the company representative what some of the biggest problems to be handled in this job are. The questions demonstrate your understanding, and the interviewer's answers outline the areas from your background and skills to which you should draw attention.

☐ *Example Five:* The interviewer will spend considerable time early in the interview describing "the type of people we *are* here at Corporation, Inc."

Response: Very simple. You have always wanted to work for a company with this atmosphere. It creates the type of work environment that is conducive to a person really giving his or her best efforts.

☐ *Example Six:* The interviewer will ask you closed-ended questions. These questions demand no more than a "yes/no" answer (e.g., "Do you pay attention to detail?"). These questions are hardly adequate to establish your skills, yet you must handle them effectively to secure the job offer.

Response: A yes/no answer to a closed-ended question will not get you that offer. The trick is to treat each closed-ended question as if the company representative has added, "Please give me a brief yet thorough answer." Closed-ended questions are often mingled with statements followed by pauses. In this instance, agree with the statement in a way that demonstrates both a grasp of your job and the interviewer's statement. For example: "That's an excellent point, Mr. Smith, I couldn't agree more that the attention to detail you describe naturally affects cost containment. My track record in this area . . ."

☐*Example Seven:* The interviewer asks a continuing stream of negative questions (as described in "Negatives and Tricks").

Response: Use the techniques and answers described earlier. Give your answers with a smile and do not take these questions as personal insults; they are not intended that way. The more stressful the situations the job is likely to place you in, the greater the likelihood of having to field negative questions. The interviewer wants to know if you can take the heat.

☐ *Example Eight:* The interviewer has difficulty looking at you while speaking.

Response: The interviewer is someone who finds it uncomfortable being in the spotlight. Try to help him or her to be a good audience. Ask specific questions about the job responsibilities and offer your skills in turn: "Would it be of value to you if I described . . ."

□ □ □

Often a hiring manager will arrange for you to meet with two or three other people. Frequently, these other interviewers have neither been trained in the appropriate interviewing skills nor told the details of the job for which you are interviewing. So you will take additional copies of your Executive Briefing with you to the interview to aid these additional interviewers in focusing on the appropriate job functions.

When you understand how to recognize and respond to these different types of interviewer, you will leave your interview having made a favorable first impression. No one forgets first impressions.

14.
The Stress Interview

For all intents and purposes, every interview is a stress interview, and is stressful by its very nature: The interviewer's questions can act merely as the catalyst for your own fear. And the only way to combat this fear is to be prepared, to know what the interviewer is trying to do, to anticipate the various tacks he or she will take. Indeed, that is why you are reading *Knock 'em Dead* in the first place, because preparedness is what will keep you cool and collected. Whenever you are ill-prepared for an interview, no one will be able to put more pressure on you than yourself.

This chapter is about the narrower definition of the stress interview, but everything you have learned in *Knock 'em Dead* applies, and all the techniques you now understand will see you through. Remember: A "stress" interview is just a regular interview with the volume turned all the way up; the music's the same, just louder.

□ □ □

You've heard the horror stories. An interviewer demands, "Sell me this pen," or asks, "How would you improve the design of a teddy bear?" Or you are faced with a battery of interviewers, all rapid-firing questions like, "You're giving a dinner party. Which ten famous people would you invite and why?" and one interviewer asking, "Living or dead?" while another sneers, "Ten of each."

Previously restricted to the executive suite for the selection of high-powered executives, stress interviews are now established throughout the professional world. And they can come complete with all the intimidating and treacherous tricks your worst dreams can devise. Yet your good performance at a stress interview can mean the difference between life in the corporate fast-lane and a stalled career. The questioners in a stress interview are experienced and well-organized, with tightly structured procedures and advanced interviewing techniques. The questions and tension they generate have the cumulative effect of throwing you off-balance and revealing the "real" you rather than someone who can respond with last night's rehearsed answers to six or seven stock questions.

One stress interview technique is to set you up for a fall: A pleasant conversation, one or a series of seemingly inocuous questions to relax your guard, then a dazzling series of jabs and body-blows that leave you gibbering. For instance, an interviewer might lull you into a false sense of security by asking some relatively stressless questions: "What was your initial starting salary at your last job?" then, "What is your salary now?" then, "Do you receive bonuses?" etc. To put you on the ropes, he or she then completely surprises you with "Tell me what sort of troubles you have living within your means." Such interviewers are using stress in an intelligent fashion, to simulate the unexpected and sometimes tense events of everyday business life. Seeing how you handle simulated pressure gives a fair indication of how you will react to the real thing.

The sophisticated interviewer talks very little, perhaps only 20% of the time, and that time is spent asking questions. Few comments, and no editorializing, on your answers, means that you get no hint, verbal or otherwise, about your performance.

The questions are planned, targeted, sequenced and layered. The interviewer covers one subject thoroughly before moving on. Let's take the simple example of "Can you work under pressure?" As a reader of *Knock 'em Dead,* you will know to answer this question with an example, and thereby deflect the main thrust of the stress technique. The interviewer will be prepared for a simple yes/no answer, and what follows is how he or she will keep the unprepared reeling.

☑ *"Can you work under pressure?"* A simple, closed-ended question that requires just a yes/no answer, but you don't get off so easy.

☐ *"Good, I'd be interested to hear about a time when you experienced pressure on your job."* An open-ended request to tell a story about a pressure situation. After this, you will be subjected to the layering technique, six layers in the following instance. Imagine how tangled you could get without preparation.

☐ *"Why do you think this situation arose?"*

☐ *"When exactly did this happen?"* (Watch out! Your story of saving thousands from the burning skyscraper may well be checked with your references.)

☐ *"What in hindsight were you most dissatisfied with about your performance?"* Here we go. You're trying to show how well you perform under pressure, then suddenly you're telling tales against yourself.

☐ *"How do you feel others could have acted more responsibly?"* An open invitation to criticize peers and superiors, which you should diplomatically decline.

☐ *"Who holds the responsibility for this occurrence?"* Another invitation to point the finger of blame.

☐ *"Where in the chain of command can steps be taken to avoid this sort of thing happening again?"*

You have just been through an old reporters' technique of asking why, when, who, what, and where. This technique can be applied to any question you are asked and is frequently used to probe those success stories that sound just too good to be true. You'll find them suddenly tagged on to the simple close-ended questions as well as to the open-ended ones, starting, "Share with me . . . ," "Tell me about a time when . . . ," or, "I'm interested in finding out about . . . ,"and requesting specific examples from your work history.

After you've survived this barrage, a friendly tone will conceal another zinger: "What did you learn from the experience?" It's a question that is geared to probing your judgment and emotional maturity. Your answer will be to emphasize whichever of the key personality traits your story was illustrating.

□ □ □

When the interviewer feels you were on the edge of revealing something unusual in an answer, "mirror statements" will be employed. There, the last key phrase of your answer will be repeated or paraphrased, and followed by a steady gaze and silence: "So, you learned that organization is the key to management." The idea is that the quiet and expectant look will work together to make you continue talking. It can give you a most disconcerting feeling to find yourself rambling on without quite knowing why. The trick to this is knowing when to stop. When the interviewer gives you the expectant look, expand your answer (you have to), but by no more that a couple of sentences. Otherwise, you will get that creepy feeling that you're digging yourself another hole.

There will be times when you face more than one interviewer at a time. When it happens, remember the story of one woman who had five interviewers all asking questions at the same time. As the poor interviewee got halfway through one answer, another question would be shot at her. Pausing for breath, she smiled and said, "Hold your horses. These are all excellent questions, and given time, I'll answer them all. Now who's next?" In so doing, she showed the interviewers exactly what they wanted to see and what, incidentally, is behind every stress interview: the search for poise and calm under fire, combined with a refusal to be intimidated.

You never know when a stress interview will raise its ugly head. Often it can be that rubber-stamp meeting with the senior V.P. at the end of a series of grueling meetings. This is not always surprising: While other interviewers are concerned with determining whether you are able, willing and manageable for the job in question, the senior executive who eventually throws you for a loop is the one who is probing you for potential promotability.

The most intimidating stress interviews are recognizable before the interviewer speaks: No eye contact, no greeting, either silence or a noncommittal grunt, no small talk and a general air of boredom, disinterest or thinly veiled aggression. The first words you hear could well be "O.K., so go ahead. I don't have all day." In these situations, forewarned is forearmed, so here are some of the questions you can expect to follow such openings.

☐ *"See this pen I'm holding? Sell it to me."*

Not a request, as you might think, that would be asked only of a salesperson. In today's business world, everyone is required to sell—sometimes products, but more often ideas, approaches, and concepts. As such, you are being tested to see whether you understand the basic concepts of Features and Benefits. For example, the interviewer holds up a broad-tip yellow highlighter. You say calmly, "Let me tell you about the special features of this product. First of all, it's a highlighter that will emphasize important points in reports or articles, and that will save you time in recalling the important features. The casing is wide enough to enable you to use it comfortably at your desk or on a flip chart. It has a flat base you can stand it up on. At one dollar, it is disposable and cheap enough to have a handful for your desk, briefcase, car and at home. And the bright yellow color means you'll never lose it."

☐ *"What is the worst thing you have heard about our company?"*

If you have heard anything truly bad about the outfit, you shouldn't be there in the first place, so it is safe to assume you haven't. Regardless, the question comes as a shock. As for all stress questions, your poise under stress is vital: If you can carry off a halfway decent answer as well, you are a winner. The best response to this question is simple: "You're a tough company to get into because your interviews and interviewers are so rigorous." It's true, it's flattering, and it shows that you are not intimidated.

☑ *"How would you define your profession?"*

With questions that solicit your understanding of a topic, no matter how good your answer, you can expect to be interrupted in mid-reply with "That has nothing to do with it," or, "Whoever put *that* idea into your head?" While your response is a judgment call, 999 times out of a thousand these comments are not meant to be taken as serious criticisms. Rather, they are tests to see how well you would be able to defend your position in a no-holds-barred conversation with the Chairman of the Board who says exactly what he or she thinks at all times. So go ahead and defend yourself, without taking or showing offense.

Your first response will be to gain time and get the interviewer talking. "Why do you say that?" you ask, answering a question with a question. And turning the tables on your aggressor displays your poise, calm, and analytical skills better than any other response.

☐ *"How would you evaluate me as an interviewer?"*

The question is dangerous, maybe more so than the one asking you to criticize your boss. Whatever you do, don't tell the truth if you think the interviewer is an unconscious incompetent. It may be true, but it won't get you a job offer. It is an instance where honesty is not the best policy. It is best to say, "This is one of the toughest interviews I have ever been through, and I don't relish the prospect of going through another. Yet I do realize what you are trying to achieve." Then go on to explain that you know there is pressure on the job and that the interviewer is trying to simulate some of that real-life pressure in the interview. You may choose to finish the answer with a question of your own: "How do you think I performed under your questioning?"

☐ *"What would you say if I told you your presentation this afternoon was lousy?"*

Of course the true stress interviewer, being competent in this trade, will come back and answer your question with a question in a way you would never expect. *If* is the key here, with the accusation only there for the terminally neurotic. The question is designed to see how you react to criticism, and so tests manageability. No company can afford the thin-skinned today.

An appropriate response to this one would be: "My first step would be to find out where you felt the problem was. If there'd been miscommunication, I'd clear it up. If the problem were elsewhere, I would seek your advice and be sure that the problem was not recurrent." This would show that when it is a manager's duty to criticize performance, you are an employee who will respond in a businesslike and emotionally mature manner.

□ □ □

Stress interviewers may pull all kinds of tricks on you, but you will come through with flying colors once you realize that they're trying to discover something extremely simple: Whether or not you can take the heat. After all, these interviewers are only trying to sort out the good corporate warriors from the walking wounded. Stay calm, give as good as you get and take it all in good part; no one can intimidate you without your permission.

15.
Strange Venues

Why are some interviews conducted in strange places? Are meetings in noisy, distracting hotel lobbies designed as a form of torture? What are the real reasons that an interviewer invites you to eat at a fancy restaurant?

For the most part, these tough-on-the-nerves situations happen because the interviewer is a busy person, fitting you into a busy schedule. Take the case of a man I know. He had heard stories about tough interview situations but never expected to face one himself. It happened at a retail convention in Arizona, and he had been asked to meet for a final interview by the pool. The interviewer was there, taking a short break between meetings, in his bathing suit. And the first thing the interviewer did was suggest that my friend slip into something into comfortable.

This scenario may not lurk in your future, but the chances are that you will face many tough interviewer situations in your career. They call for a clear head and a little gamesmanship to put you ahead of the competition. The interviewee at the pool used both. He removed his pinstripe jacket, folded it over the arm of the chair and seated himself, saying pleasantly, "That's much better. Where shall we begin?"

It isn't easy to remain calm at times like these. On top of interview nerves, you're worried about being overhead in a public place, or (worse) surprised by the appearance of your current boss. That last item isn't too far-fetched. It actually happened to a reader from San Francisco. She was being interviewed in the departure lounge at the airport when her boss walked through the arrivals door. Oops! (She had asked for the day off "to take the dog to the vet.")

Could she have avoided the situation? Certainly, if she had asked about privacy when the meeting was arranged. This would have reminded the interviewer of the need for discretion. The point is to do all you can in advance to make such a meeting as private as possible. Once that's done, you can ignore the rest of the world and concentrate on the interviewer's questions.

□ □ □

Hotel Lobbies and Other Strange Places

Strange interview situations provide other wonderful opportunities to embarrass yourself. You come to a hotel lobby in full corporate battle dress: coat, briefcase, perhaps an umbrella. You sit down to wait for the interviewer. "Aha," you think to yourself, opening your briefcase, "I'll show him my excellent work habits by delving into this computer printout."

That's not such a great idea. Have you ever tried rising with your lap covered with business papers, then juggling the briefcase from right hand to left to accommodate the ritual handshake? It's quite difficult. Besides, while sitting in nervous anticipation, pre-interview tension has no way of dissipating. Your mouth will become dry, and your "Good morning, I'm pleased to meet you" will come out strained.

To avoid such catastrophes in places like hotel lobbies, first remove your coat on arrival. Then, instead of sitting, walk around a little while you wait. Even in a small lobby, a few steps back and forth will help you reduce tension to a manageable level. Keep your briefcase in your left hand at all times; it makes you look purposeful, and you won't trip over it when you meet the interviewer.

If, for any reason, you must sit down, make a conscious effort to breathe deeply and slowly. This will help control the adrenaline that makes you feel jumpy.

A strange setting can actually put you on equal footing with the interviewer. Neither of you is on home turf, so in many cases, the interviewer will feel just as awkward as you do. A little gamesmanship can turn the occasion to your advantage.

To gain the upper hand, get to the meeting site early to scout the territory. By knowing your surroundings, you will feel more relaxed. Early arrival also allows you control the outcome of the meeting in other subtle ways. You will have time to stake out the most private spot in an otherwise public place. Corners are best. They tend to be quieter, and you can choose the seat that puts your back to the wall (in a practical sense, that is). In this position, you have a clear view of your surroundings and will feel more secure. The fear of being overheard will evaporate.

The situation is now somewhat in your favor. You know the locale, and the meeting place is as much yours as the interviewer's. You will have a clear view of your surroundings, and odds are that you will be more relaxed than the interviewer. When he or she arrives, say, "I arrived a little early to make sure we had some privacy. I think over here is the best spot." With this positive demonstration of your organizational abilities, you give yourself a head start over the competition.

□ □ □

The Meal Meeting

Breakfast, lunch, or dinner are the prime choices for interviewers who want to catch the seasoned professional off-guard. In fact, the meal is arguably the toughest of all tough interview situations. The setting offers the interviewer the chance to see you in a non-office (and therefore more natural) setting, to observe your social graces and see you as a whole person. Here, topics that would be impossible to address in the traditional office setting will naturally surface, often with virtually no effort on the part of the interviewer. The slightest slip in front of that wily old sea pirate opposite—thinly disguised in a Brooks Brothers suit—could get your candidacy deep-sixed quickly.

Usually, you will not be invited to a dinner meetings until you have already demonstrated that you are capable of doing the job. It's a good sign, actually: An invitation to a meal means that you are under strong consideration, and, by extension, intense scrutiny.

This meeting is often the final hurdle, and could lead directly to the job offer—assuming, of course, that you handle properly the occasional surprises that arise. The interviewer's concern is not whether you can do the job, but whether you have the growth potential that will allow you to fill more senior slots as they become available.

You can still blow it. Being interviewed in front of others is bad enough; eating and drinking in front of them at the same time only makes it worse. If you knock over a glass or dribble spaghetti sauce down your chin, the interviewer will be so busy smirking that he or she won't hear what you have to say.

□ □ □

To be sure that the interviewer remains as attentive to the positive points of your candidacy as possible, let's discuss table manners.

Your social graces and general demeanor at the table can tell as much about you as your answer to a question. For instance, over-ordering food or drink can signal poor self-discipline. At the very least, it will call into question your judgment and maturity. High-handed behavior toward waiters and buspersons could reflect negatively on your ability to get along with subordinates and on your leadership skills. These concerns are amplified when you return food or complain about the service, actions which, at the very least, find fault with the interviewer's choice of restaurant.

By the same token, you will want to observe how your potential employer behaves. After all, you are likely to become an employee, and the interviewer's table manners can tell you a lot about what it will be like on the job.

□ *Alcohol*

Soon after being seated, you will be offered a drink—if not by your host, then by the waiter. There are many reasons to avoid alcohol at interview meals. The most important reason is that alcohol fuzzes your mind, and research proves that stress increases the intoxicating effect of alcohol. So, if you order something to drink, try to stick with something non-alcoholic, such as a club soda or simply a glass of water. If pressed, order a white-wine spritzer, a sherry, or a beer—it depends on the environment and what your host is drinking.

If you do have a drink, never have more than one. If there is a bottle of wine on the table, and the waiter offers you another glass, simply place your hand over the top of the glass. It is a polite way of signifying no.

You may be offered alcohol at the end of the meal. The rule still holds true—turn it down. You need your wits about you even if the interview seems to be drawing to a close. Some interviewers will try to use these moments, when your defenses are at their lowest, to throw in a couple of zingers.

☐ Smoking

Smoking is another big problem that is best handled by taking a simple approach. Don't do it unless encouraged. If both of you are smokers, and you are encouraged to smoke, follow a simple rule: Never smoke between courses, only at the end of a meal. Most confirmed nicotine addicts, like the rest of the population, hate smoke while they are eating.

☐ Utensils

Keep all your cups and glasses at the top of your place setting and well away from you. Most glasses are knocked over at a cluttered table when one stretches for the condiments or gesticulates to make a point. Of course, your manners will prevent you from reaching rudely for the pepper-shaker.

When you are faced with an array of knives, forks, and spoons, it is always safe to start at the outside and work your way in as the courses come. Keep your elbows at your sides and don't slouch in the chair. When pausing between mouthfuls (which, if your are promoting yourself properly, should be frequently), rest your knife and fork on the plate this way.

The time to start eating, of course, is when the interviewer does; the time to stop is when he or she does. At the end of a course or the meal, rest your knife and fork together on the plate, at five o'clock.

Here are some other helpful hints:

□ Of course, you should never speak with your mouth full.

□ To be on the safe side, eat the same thing, or close to it, as the interviewer. Of course, this rule may make sense in theory, but the fact is that you will probably be asked to order first, so ordering the same thing can become problematic. Solve the problem before you order by complimenting the restaurant during your small talk and then, when the menus arrive, asking, "What do think you will have today?"

□ Do not change your order once it is made, and never send the food back.

□ Be polite to your waiters, even when they spill soup in your lap.

□ Don't order expensive food. Naturally, in our heart of hearts, we all like to eat well, especially on someone else's tab. But don't be tempted. When you come right down to it, you are there to talk and be seen at your best, not to eat.

□ Eat what you know. Stay away from awkward, messy, or exotic foods (e.g., artichokes, long pasta, and escargot, respectively). Ignore finger foods, such as lobster or spare ribs. In fact, you should avoid eating with your fingers altogether, unless you are in a sand-wich joint, in which case you should make a point of avoiding the leaky, over-stuffed menu items.

□ Don't order salad. The dressing can often get messy. If a salad comes with the meal, request that the dress-ing be on the side. Then, before pouring it on, cut the lettuce up first.

□ Don't order anything with bones. Stick with filets; there are few simple, gracious ways to deal with any type of bone.

□ *Checks and Goodbyes*

I know an interviewer who hires high-ticket, business-to-business salespeople. Her favorite test of composure is to have the waiter, by arrangement, put the bill on the interviewee's side of the table. She then chats on, waiting for something interesting to happen. If you ever find yourself in a similar situation, never pick up the check, however long it is left by your plate. When ready, your host will pick it up—that's the simple protocol of the occasion. By the same token, you should never offer to share payment.

When parting company, always thank the host for his or her hospitality and the wonderful meal. Of course, you should be sure to leave on a positive note by asking good-naturedly what you have to do to get the job.

Strange interview situations can arise at any time during the interview cycle, and in any public place. Wherever you are asked to go, keep your guard up. Your table manners, listening skills, and overall social graces are being judged. The question on the interviewer's mind is: Can you be trusted to represent the company graciously?

16.
Welcome to the Real World

Of all the steps a school-leaver will take up the ladder of success over the years, none is more important or more difficult than getting a foot on the first rung. And the interviewing processes designed for recent graduates are particularly rigorous, because management regards the hiring of entry-level professionals as one of its toughest jobs.

When a company hires experienced people, there is a track record to evaluate. With school-leavers, there is little or nothing. Often, the only solid things an interviewer has to go on are high school, SAT, and college grades. That's not much on which to base a hiring decision: Grades don't tell the interviewer whether you will fit in or make a reliable employee. Many recruiters liken the gamble of hiring recent graduates to laying down wines for the future. They know that some will develop into full-bodied, reliable vintages, but that others will be disappointments. So, recruiters have to find different ways to predict potential accurately.

After relying, as best they can, on school performance to evaluate your ability, interviewers concentrate on questions that reveal how willing you are to learn and get the job done, and how manageable you are likely to be on average days and when the going gets rough.

Your goal is to stand out from all the other entry-level candidates as someone altogether different and better. For example, don't be like thousands of others who, in answer to questions about their greatest strength, reply lamely, "I'm good with people" or, "I like working with others." As you know by now, such answers do not separate you from the herd. In fact, they brand you as *average*. To stand out, a school-leaver must recount a past situation that *illustrates* how good he or she is with people, or one that demonstrates an ability to be a team player. Fortunately, the key personality traits discussed throughout the book are just as helpful for getting your foot on the ladder as they are for aiding you in your climb to the top. They will guide you in choosing what aspects of your personality and background you should promote at the interview.

It isn't necessary to have snap answers ready for every question, because you never will. In fact, it is more important for you to pause after a question and collect your thoughts before answering: You must show that you think before you speak. That way, you will demonstrate your analytical abilities, which age feels youth has in short supply.

By the same token, occasionally asking for a question to be repeated is useful to gain time and is quite acceptable, as long as you don't do it with *every* question. And if a question stumps you, as sometimes happens, do not stutter incoherently. It is sometimes best to say simply, "I don't know." Or, you might say, "I'd like to come back to that later," because the odds are even that the interviewer will forget to ask again; if not, at least you've had some time to come up with an answer.

Knowing *everything* about a certain entry-level position is not necessary, because business feels it can teach you most things. But, as a vice president of Merrill Lynch once said, "You must bring to the table the ability to speak clearly." So, knowing what is behind those questions designed especially for school-leavers will give you the time to build informative and understandable answers.

□ *"How did you get your summer jobs?"*

All employers look favorably on recent graduates who have any work experience, no matter what it is. "It is far easier to get a fix on someone who has worked while at school," says Dan O'Brien, head of employment at Grumman Aerospace. "They manage their time better, are more realistic and more mature. Any work experience gives us much more in common." So, as you make your answer, add that you learned that business is about making a profit, doing things more efficiently, adhering to procedures, and putting out whatever effort it takes to get the job done. In short, treat your summer jobs, no matter how humble, as any other business experience.

In this particular question, the interviewer is looking ideally for something that shows initiative, creativity, and flexibility. Here's an example: "In my town, summer jobs were hard to come by, but I applied to each local restaurant for a position waiting tables, called the manager at each one to arrange an interview, and finally landed a job at one of the most prestigious. I was assigned to the afternoon shift, but with my quick work, accurate billing, and ability to keep customers happy, they soon moved me to the evening shift. I worked there for three summers, and by the time I left, I was responsible for the training and management of the night-shift waiters, the allotment of tips, and the evening's final closing and accounting. All in all, my experience showed me the mechanics of a small business and of business in general."

☐ *"Which of the jobs you've held have you liked least?"*

The interviewer is trying to trip you up. It is likely that your work experience contained a certain amount of repetition and drudgery, as all early jobs in the business world do. So beware of saying that you hated a particular job "because it was boring." Avoid the negative and say something along these lines: "All of my jobs had their good and bad points, but I've always found that if you want to learn, there's plenty to be picked up every day. Each experience was valuable."

☐ *"What are your future vocational plans?"*

This is a fancy way of asking, "Where do you want to be five years from now?" The trap all entry-level professionals make is to say, "In management," because they think that shows drive and ambition. It has become such a trite answer, though, that it immediately generates a string of questions that most recent graduates can't answer: What is the definition of management? what is a manager's prime responsibility? a manager in what area? Your safest answer identifies you with the profession into which you are trying to break. "In five years or so, I hope to have become a thorough professional with a clear understanding of the company, the industry, and where the opportunities really lie. By that time, my goals for the future should be sharply defined." An answer like that will set you far apart from your contemporaries.

□ *"Are you looking for a permanent or temporary job?"*

The interviewer wants reassurance that you are genuinely interested in the position and won't disappear in a few months without notice. Try to go beyond saying simply yes: Explain why you want the job. You might say, "Of course, I am looking for a permanent job. I intend to make my career in this field, and I want the opportunity to learn the business, face new challenges, and learn from experienced professionals."

□ *"We have tried to hire people from your school/your major before, and they never seem to work out. What makes you different?"*

Here's a stress question to test your poise and analytical skills. You can shout that, yes, of *course* you are different and can prove it, but so far, all you know is that there was a problem, not what caused the problem. Respond this way: "First, may I ask you exactly what problems you've had with people from this background?" Once you know what the problem is (if one really exists at all), then you can illustrate how you are different—but only then. Otherwise, you run the risk of your answer being interrupted with, "Well, that's what everyone else said before I hired them. You haven't shown me that you are any different."

□ *"Do you like routine tasks/regular hours?"*

A trick question. The interviewer knows from bitter experience that most school-leavers hate routine and are hopeless as employees until they come to an acceptance of such facts of life. Explain that, yes, you appreciate the need for routine, that you expect a fair amount of routine assignments before you are entrusted with the more responsible ones, and that is why you are prepared to accept it as necessary. As far as regular hours go, you could say, "No, there's no problem there. A company expects to make a profit, so the doors have to be open for business on a regular basis."

☑ *"What have you done that shows initiative and willingness to work?"*

Again, tell a story about how you landed or created a job for yourself, or even got involved in some volunteer work. Your answer should show initiative in that you both handled unexpected problems calmly and anticipated others. Your willingness is demonstrated by the ways you overcame obstacles. For example: "I worked for a summer in a small warehouse. I found out that a large shipment was due in a couple of weeks, and I knew that room had to be made. The inventory system was outdated, and the rear of the warehouse was disorganized, so I came in on a Saturday, figured out how much room I needed, cleaned up the mess in the rear, and catalogued it all on new inventory forms. When the shipment arrived, the truck just backed in. There was even room to spare."

☐ *"Can you take instructions without feeling upset or hurt?"*

This is a manageability question. If you take offense easily or bristle when your mistakes are pointed out, you won't last long with any company. Competition is fierce at the entry level, so take this as another chance to set yourself apart. "Yes, I can take instructions, and more important, I can take constructive criticism without feeling hurt. Even with the best intent, I will still make mistakes and at times someone will have to put me back on the right track. I know that if I ever expect to rise in the company, I must first prove myself to be manageable."

☐ *"Have you ever had difficulties getting along with others?"*

This is a combination question, probing willingness and manageability. Are you a team player or are you going to disrupt the department and make the interviewer's life hell? This is a closed-ended question that requires only a yes/no answer, so give one and shut up.

☐ *"What type of position are you interested in?"*

This again is one of those questions that tempts you to say management. Don't. Say you are interested in what you will be offered anyway, which is an entry-level job. "I am interested in an entry-level position that will enable me to learn this business inside and out, and will give me the opportunity to grow when I prove myself.''

□ *"What qualifications do you have that will make you successful in this field?''*

To answer this is just a matter of illustrating your strong points as they match the key personality traits in Chapter 10, and as they apply to the position you seek. It's a simple, wide-open question that says, "Hey, we're looking for an excuse to hire you. Give us some help.''

□ *"Why do you think you would like this type of work?''*

This is a deceptively simple question because there is no pat answer. It is usually asked to see whether you really understand what the specific job and profession entails on a day-to-day basis. So, to answer it requires you to have researched the company and job functions as carefully as possible. Preparation for this should include a call to another company in the field and asking to speak to someone doing the job you hope to get. Ask what the job is like and what that person does day-to-day. How does the job fit into the department? what contribution does it make to the overall efforts of the company? why does he or she like this type of work? Armed with this information, you will show that you understand what you are getting into; most recent graduates do not.

□ *"What's your idea of how industry works?''*

The interviewer does not want a long dissertation, just the reassurance that you don't think it works along the same lines as a registered charity. Your understanding should be something like this: "The role of any company is to make as much money as possible, as quickly and efficiently as possible, and in a manner that will encourage repeat business from the existing client base and new business from word of mouth and reputation.'' Finish with the observation that it is every employee's role to play their part as a team member in order to achieve these goals.

□ *"What do you know about our company?''*

You can't answer this question unless you have enough interest to research the company thoroughly. If you don't, you should expect someone who has made the effort to get the job.

☐ *"What do you think determines progress in a good company?"*

Your answer will include all the positive personality traits you have been illustrating throughout the interview. Include allusions to the listening profile, determination, ability to take the rough with the smooth, and the good fortune to have a manager who wants you to grow.

☐ *"Do you think grades should be considered by first employers?"*

If your grades were good, the answer is obviously yes. If they weren't, your answer needs a little more thought. "Of course, an employer should take everything into consideration, and along with grades will be an evaluation of willingness, manageability, an understanding of how business works, and actual work experience. These things combined can can be more valuable than grades alone."

☐ ☐ ☐

Many virtuous candidates are called for entry-level interviews, but only those who prepare themselves to answer the tougher questions will be chosen. Interviews for school-leavers are partly sales presentations. And the more you interview, the better you get, so don't leave preparing for them until the last minute. Start now and hone your skills to get a head start on your peers. Finally, here's what a professor from a top-notch business school once told me: "You are taking a new product to market. So, you've got to analyze what it can do, who is likely to be interested, and how you are going to sell it to them."

17.
The Newest Questions From Today's Toughest Interviewers

The ingenuity of interviewers' questions never ceases to amaze me. Over the last year, readers of *Knock 'em Dead* or attendees of my seminars have come up with some questions that are real stinkers. They say, "O.K., you're so smart. How do you answer *this* one?" Well, to some of the toughest questions, there is never a "right" answer—that's what makes them the toughest—but there is always a right approach. So, here are some of the current crop of tough questions and the best approaches for those higher-level jobs.

□ *"What are the broad responsibilities of a [e.g.] systems analyst?"*

This is suddenly becoming a very popular question with interviewers, and rightly so. There are three layers to it. First, it acknowledges that all employees are nowadays required to be more efficiency- and profit-conscious. Second, the answer provides some idea of how much you will have to be taught or reoriented if and when you join the company. Third, it is a very effective knock-out question—if you lack a comprehensive understanding of your job, that's it, you'll be knocked out then and there. So, while your answer must reflect an understanding of the responsibilities, be wary of falling afoul of differing corporate jargon. A systems analyst in one company, for instance, may be only a programmer trainee in another. With this in mind, you may wish to preface your answer with

"While the responsibilities of my job title vary somewhat from company to company, at my current/last job, my responsibilities included . . . " Then, in case you unwittingly trip yourself up in the answer, finish with a question: "How do those responsibilities match the ones here?" This will give you the opportunity to recoup any mistakes.

☑ *"Describe how your job relates to the overall goals of your department and company."*

This probes not only your understanding of department and corporate missions, but also obliquely checks into your ability to function as a team member to get the work done. Consequently, whatever the specifics of your answer, include words to this effect: "The quality of my work directly affects the ability of others to do their work properly. As a team member, one has to be aware of the other players."

☑ *"What aspects of your job do you consider most crucial?"*

A wrong answer can knock you out of the running in short order. The salesperson who describes expense reports as the job's most crucial aspect is a case in point. The question is designed to determine time management, prioritization skills, and any inclination for task avoidance.

☐ *"What is an adequate reward for your efforts?"*

A glaring manageability question. The interviewer probably already has a typist on staff who expects a Nobel prize each time she gets out a faultless letter. Your answer should be honest and cover all bases. "My primary satisfaction and reward comes from a job well done and completed on time. The occasional good word from my boss is always welcome. Last but not least, I think everyone looks forward to a salary review."

☑ *"With hindsight, how could you have improved your progress?"*

Here's a question that says, "Tell me your mistakes and weaknesses." If you can mention ways of improving your performance without damaging your candidacy, do so. The end of your answer should be something like: "Other than that, I don't know what to add. I have always given it my best shot." Then shut up.

☑ *"What area of your skills/professional development do you want to improve at this time?"*

Another particularly adroit way of asking you to reveal key weaknesses. The safest response is to reiterate one or two areas that combine personal strengths and the job's most crucial responsibilities, and finish with saying, "These areas are so important that I don't think anyone can be too good, or should ever stop trying to polish his or her skills."

☑ *"What kinds of things do you worry about?"*

Some questions, such as this one, can seem so off-the-wall that you might start treating the interviewer as a father confessor in no time flat. Your private phobias have nothing to do with your job, and revealing them can get you labeled as unbalanced. It is best to confine your answer to the sensible worries of a conscientious professional. "I worry about deadlines, staff turnover, tardiness, back-up plans for when the computer crashes, or that one of my salespeople burns out or defects to the competition—just the normal stuff. It goes with the territory, so I don't let it get me down."

☑ *"What is the most difficult situation you have faced?"*

The question looks for information on two fronts: How do you define difficult? and, what was your handling of the situation? You must have a story ready for this one in which the situation both was tough and allowed you to show yourself in a good light. Avoid talking about problems that have to do with coworkers.

☐ *"What are some of the things that bother you? What are your pet hates? Tell me about the last time you felt anger on the job."*

These questions are so similar that they can be treated here as one. It is tremendously important that you show you can remain calm. Most of us have seen a colleague lose his or her cool on occasion—not a pretty sight and one that every sensible employer wants to avoid. This question comes up more and more often the higher up the corporate ladder you climb and the more frequent your contact with clients and the general public. To answer it, find something that angers conscientious workers. "I enjoy my work and believe in giving value to my employer. Dealing with clock-watchers and the ones who regularly get sick on Mondays and Fridays really bothers me, but it's not something that gets me *angry* or anything like that." An answer of this nature will help you much more than the kind given by a California engineer, who went on for some minutes about how he hated the small-mindedness of people who don't like pet rabbits—in the office.

□ *"What is the least relevant job you have held?"*

If your least relevant job is not on your resume, it shouldn't be mentioned. Some people skip over those six months between jobs when they worked as soda jerks just to pay the bills, and would rather not talk about it, until they hear a question like this. But a mention of a job that, according to all chronological records, you never had, will throw your integrity into question and your candidacy out the door.

Apart from that, no job in your profession has been a waste of time if it increases your knowledge about how the business works and makes money. Your answer will include, "Every job I've held has given me new insights into my profession, and the higher one climbs, the more important the understanding of the lower-level, more menial jobs. They all play a role in making the company profitable. And anyway, it's certainly easier to schedule and plan work when you have first-hand knowledge of what others will have to do to complete their tasks."

☑ *"Explain your role as a group/team member."*

You are being asked to describe yourself as either a team player or a loner. Most departments depend on harmonious teamwork for their success, so describe yourself as a team player, by all means: "I perform my job in a way that helps others to do theirs in an efficient fashion. Beyond the mechanics, we all have a responsibility to make the workplace a friendly and pleasant place to be. That means everyone working for the common good and making the necessary personal sacrifices toward that good."

☑ *"How would you define a conducive work atmosphere?"*

This is a tricky question, especially because you probably have no idea what kind of work atmosphere exists in that particular office. So, the longer your answer, the greater your chances of saying the wrong thing. Keep it short and sweet. "One where the team has a genuine interest in its work and desire to turn out a good product/deliver a good service."

☑ *"How do you organize and plan for major projects?"*

Effective planning requires both forward thinking ("Who and what am I going to need to get this job done?") and backward thinking ("If this job must be completed by the 20th, what steps have to be made, and at what time, to achieve this?"). Effective planning also includes contingencies and budgets for time and cost overruns. Show that you cover all the bases.

☐ *"How many hours a week do you find it necessary to work to get your job done?"*

No absolutely correct answer, so again, you have to cover all the bases. Some managers pride themselves on working nights and weekends, on never taking their full vacation quota. Others pride themselves on their excellent planning and time management that allows them never to work more that regular office hours. You must pick the best of both worlds: "I try to plan my time effectively and usually can. Our business always has its rushes, though, so I put in whatever effort it takes to get the job finished." It is rare that the interviewer will then come back and ask for a specific number of hours. If that does happen, turn the question around: "It depends on the projects. What is typical in your department?" The answer will give you the right cue, of course.

☑ *"Tell me how you moved up through the organization."*

A fast-track question, the answer to which tells a lot about your personality, your goals, your past, your future, and whether you still have any steam left in you. The answer might be long, but try to avoid rambling. Include a fair sprinkling of your key personality traits in your stories (because this is the perfect time to do it). As well as listing the promotions, you will want to demonstrate that they came as a result of dedicated, long-term effort, substantial contributions, and flashes of genius.

☐ *"In hindsight, what have you done that was a little harebrained?"*

You are never harebrained in your business dealings and you haven't been harebrained in your personal life since graduation, right? The only safe examples to use are ones from your deep past that ultimately turned out well. One of the best to use, if it applies to you, is this one: "Well, I guess the time I bought my house. I had no idea what I was letting myself in for, and at the time, I really couldn't afford it. Still, I managed to make the payments, though I had to work like someone possessed. Yes, my first house—that was a real learning experience." Not only can most people relate to this example, but it also gives you the opportunity to sell one or two of your very positive and endearing traits.

Readers' Questions from 1987

Last year, letters arrived from my publisher almost every day. Readers of *Knock 'em Dead*, each with a specific problem, needed help. Here are some questions and situations that came up frequently.

☐ *"Why should I hire an outsider when I could fill the job with someone inside the company?"*

The question isn't as stupid as it sounds. Obviously, the interviewer has examined existing employees with an eye toward their promotion or re-assignment. Just as obviously, the job cannot be filled from within the company. If it could be, it would be, and for two very good reasons: It is cheaper for the company to promote from within, and it is good for employee morale.

Hiding behind this intimidating question is actually a pleasant invitation: "Tell me why I should hire *you*." Your answer follows two steps. The first is a simple recitation of your skills and personality profile strengths, tailored to the specific requirements of the job.

For the second step, realize first that whenever a manager is filling a position, he or she is looking not only for someone who can do the job, but also for someone who can benefit the department in a larger sense. No department is as good as it could be—each has weaknesses that need strengthening. So in the second part of your answer, include a question of your own: "Those are my general attributes. However, if no one is promotable from inside the company, that means you are looking to add strength to your team in a special way. In what ways do you hope the final candidate will be able to benefit your department?" The answer to this is your cue to sell your applicable qualities.

☐ *"Have you ever had any financial difficulties?"*

The potential employer wants to know whether you can control not only your own finances, but finances in general. If you are in the insurance field, for example—claims, accounting, supervision, management—you can expect to hear this one. The question, though, is not restricted to insurance: Anyone who handles money in day-to-day business is fair game.

Remember that for someone to check your credit history, he or she must have your written consent. This is required under the 1972 Fair Credit and Reporting Act. When you fill out an application form and sign and date it, invariably somewhere on the form is a release permitting the employer to check your credit history. If you have already filled out the form, you might not hear the question, but your creditors might.

The reader who asked me about this question went into some detail about how she had handled it during the interview. She covered, blow by blow, the whole terrible personal tragedy of her bankruptcy. In trying to be open and honest, she had done herself a disservice.

The interviewer does not want to hear sob-stories. Concentrate on the information that will damage your candidacy least and enhance it the most. You might find it appropriate to bring the matter up yourself. But, even if you choose to wait, you might say, "I should tell you that some years ago, for reasons beyond my control, I was forced into personal bankruptcy. That has been behind me for some time. Today, I have a sound credit rating and no debts. Bankruptcy is not something I'm proud of, but I did learn from the experience, and I feel it has made me a more proficient account supervisor." The answer concentrated on today, not past history.

☐ *"How ao you handle rejection?"*

This question is common if you are applying for a job in sales, including face-to-face sales, telemarketing, public relations, and customer service. If you are after a job in one of these areas and you really *don't* like the heavy doses of rejection that are any salesperson's lot, consider a new field. The anguish you will experience will not lead to a successful career or a happy life.

With that in mind, let's look behind the question. The interviewer simply wants to know whether you take rejection as rejection of yourself or whether you simply accept it as a temporary rejection of a service or product. Here is a sample answer that you can tailor to your particular needs and background: "I accept rejection as an integral part of the sales process. If everyone said yes to a product, there would be no need for the sales function. As it is, I see every rejection as bringing me closer to the customer who *will* say yes." Then, if you are encouraged to go on: "I regard rejection as simply a fact of life, that the customer has no need for the product *today*. I can go on to my next call with the conviction that I am a little closer to my next sale."

☐ *A reader writes: "I read the chapter entitled* 'Snatching Victory from the Jaws of Defeat,' *and I did everything you said to salvage what appeared to be a losing interview. My efforts did make an impression on the interviewer, but as it was explained to me, I really did not have equal qualifications for the job, and finally came in a close second. I really want to work for this growing company, and they say they have another position coming up in six months. What should I do?"*

I know of someone in the airline business who wanted a job working on that most prestigious of aircraft, the Concorde. He had been recently laid off and had high hopes for a successful interview. As it happened, he came in second for the Concorde position. He was told that the firm would speak to him again in the near future. So he waited—for eight months. Finally, he realized that waiting for the job could only leave him unemployed. The moral of the story is that you must be brutally objective when you come out second best and, whatever the interviewer says, you must sometimes assume that you are getting the polite brush-off.

With that in mind, let's see what can be done on the positive side. First of all, send a thank-you note to the interviewer, acknowledging your understanding of the state of affairs and re-affirming your desire to work for the company. Conclude with a polite request to bear you in mind for the future.

Then, keep an eye out for any news item about the company in the press. Whenever you see something, cut it out and mail it to the interviewer with a very brief note that says something like: "I came across this in *Forbes* and thought you might find it interesting. I am still determined to be your next account manager, so please keep me in mind when an opening occurs."

You can also call the interviewer once every couple of months, just to check in. Remember, of course, to keep the phone call brief and polite: You simply want to keep your name at the top of the interviewer's mind.

And maybe something will come of it. Ultimately, however, your only choice is to move on. There is no gain waiting on an interviewer's word. Go out and keep looking, because chances are that you will come up with an even better job. Then, if you still want to work for that company that gave you the brush-off, you will have some leverage.

☐ *"What do I say when the interviewer asks me whether I have any questions?"*

A good question. Almost always, this is a sign that the interview is drawing to a close, and that you have one more chance to make an impression. Remember the old adage: People respect what you inspect, not what you expect. Create questions from any of the following:

> ☐ Find out why the job is open, who had it last, and what happened to him or her. Did he or she get promoted or fired? How many people have held this position in the last couple of years? What happened to them subsequently?
>
> ☐ Why did the interviewer join the company? How long has he or she been there? What is it about the company that keeps him or her there?
>
> ☐ To whom would you report? Will you get the opportunity to meet that person?
>
> ☐ Where is the job located? What are the travel re quirements, if any?

☐ What type of training is required, and how long is it? What type of training is available?

☐ What would your first assignment be?

☑ What are the realistic chances for growth in the job? Where are the opportunities for greatest growth within the company?

☐ What are the skills and attributes most needed to get ahead in the company?

☐ Who will be the company's major competitor over the next few years? How does the interviewer feel the company stacks up against them?

☐ What has been the growth pattern of the company over the last five years: Is it profitable? How profitable? Is the company privately or publicly held?

☐ If there is a written job description, may you see it?

☐ How regularly do performance evaluations occur? What model do they follow?

☐ *A reader writes: "About 18 years ago, I had a bright future in the business world as a personal assistant to the president of a large company. Then, I got married, left the workplace for a couple of years, and started a family. Now, interviewers are saying that my experience is irrelevant in today's marketplace. What can I do?"*

Unfortunately, some employers look askance at returnees to the workplace. They believe that skills have either atrophied or are now inappropriate. If you don't have current business-world experience, the interviewer may not think that he or she has much to discuss with you. Employers also may think that there will be lifestyle and time-management adjustment problems for you. It is difficult, often impossible, to get the chance to shine with this closed-minded interviewer, even if you are better today than you were back then.

If you are re-entering the job market, you can deflect the interviewer's doubts by taking a short stint in the wonderful world of temps. Working for a temporary help agency (which *will* recognize your skills) will get you rapid exposure to diverse corporate cultures and varied jobs. Most important, you will receive constant career coaching from the temp company.

Although not all temporary companies encourage their temps to become permanent employees with client companies, you will have the opportunity to be on-site and to see the permanent jobs as they become available. Also, if you do a good job with a client company, there is a reasonable chance that the employer will create a position for you.

☐ *"How should I handle an illegal question?"*

Title VII is a federal law that forbids employers to discriminate against any person on the basis of sex, age, race, national origin, or religion. In addition, many states have laws that protect people who fall into other categories, such as the physically challenged.

But what is an illegal question? Employment discrimination, as illegal and unsavory as it is, is difficult to pinpoint, and even harder to litigate. Your best bet is to go by your common sense, by what is important to you. That gives you a few options:

> ☐ *Answer the question.* If you are asked pointed questions about your ancestry, your age, or your personal life, and you want the job despite the interviewer's (and company's) apparent discriminatory bent, tell the interviewer what he or she wants to hear.

> ☐ *Say, "I don't believe that question is relevant to my ability to do the job."* If you want the job, this a good way to signal the interviewer that you are aware of what he or she is doing.

> ☐ *Ask the interviewer to explain the question's relevance to the job.* This gives you time to clarify both your choices and what the interviewer is driving at.

> ☐ *Walk out.* Say, "Thank you for your time. May I have your card?" Pocket the interviewer's business card, then say, "I want to get your name right when I report you to the Equal Employment Opportunity Commission and bring a discriminatory suit against you." There! You didn't want to work for that company anyway. On the other hand, you may find your position improved significantly—the firm might offer you a job immediately out of fear. Then you can take all the time you need to decide whether or not you want the position.

This is a complicated issue, and your response depends largely on the way you feel about the question when it is posed. To take legal action against the interviewer and the company is always an option, but that depends both on your anger and what your lawyer says. Ultimately, this book about how to answer legitimate interview questions and get the job. The subject of discriminatory questions could probably fill another volume quite easily.

Here are some guidelines, however, that interviewers must follow:

☐ An interviewer may not ask about your religion, church, synagogue, parish, the religious holidays you observe, or your political beliefs or affiliations. He or she may not ask, "Does your religion allow you to work on Saturdays?" *But*, the interviewer may ask something like, "The job requires that you work on Saturday. Is that a problem?"

☐ An interviewer may not ask about your ancestry, national origin, parentage; the naturalization status of your parents, spouse, or children; or your birthplace. *But*, the interviewer may ask (and probably will, considering the new immigration laws) whether you are a U.S. citizen or a resident alien with the right to work in the U.S.

☐ An interviewer may not ask about your native language, the language you speak at home, or how you acquired the ability to read, write, or speak a foreign language. *But*, he or she may ask about the languages in which you are fluent, if knowledge of these languages is pertinent to the job.

☐ An interviewer may not ask about your age, your date of birth, or the ages of your children. *But*, he or she may ask you whether you are over 18 years old.

☐ An interviewer may not ask about maiden names or whether you have changed your name; your marital status, number of children or dependents, or your spouse's occupation; whether you wish to be addressed as Miss, Mrs., or Ms. *But*, he or she may ask about how you like to be addressed and whether you have ever worked for the company before under a different name. (You may want to mention anyway that you have worked in other companies under a different name. That becomes important when the time comes to verify educational background, other employers, and so forth.)

You should consider, in dealing with this issue, that the interviewer is probably as nervous as you are during the interview. He or she might ask an offensive question without meaning to. Try to be polite, as you would be in any other social situation. *You* don't want to make any rash assumptions.

☑ *"Tell me about a time when you put your foot in your mouth."*

Answer this question with caution. The interviewer is examining your ability and willingness to interact pleasantly with others. The question is tricky because it asks you to show yourself in a poor light. Your answer will downplay the negative impact of your action and will end with positive information about your candidacy. The best thing to do is to start with an example outside of the workplace.

"About five years ago, I let the cat out of the bag about a surprise birthday party for a friend, a terrific *faux pas*. It was a mortifying experience, and I promised myself not to let anything like that happen again." Then, after this fairly innocuous statement, you can talk about communications in the workplace.

"As far as work is concerned, I always regard employer/employee communications on any sensitive matter as confidential unless expressly stated otherwise. So, putting my foot in my mouth doesn't happen to me at work."

□ □ □

Those were some of the more thought-provoking questions I've heard since *Knock 'em Dead* was originally published. That does not mean that there aren't more of them out there, or that more won't be devised in the future. If you are asked a question that this book does not address or show you how to handle, let me know. Send me the question, in care of the publisher, and I'll do my best to send you the answer—and perhaps include the question in the next edition.

18.
The Graceful Exit

To paraphrase Shakespeare, all the world's a stage and all the people on it merely players making their entrances and exits. Curtains rise and fall, and your powerful performance must be capped with a professional and memorable exit. To ensure you leave the right impression, this chapter will review the dos and don'ts of leaving an interview.

A signal that the interview is drawing to a close comes when you are asked whether you have any final questions. Ask your own questions, and by doing so, highlight your strengths and show your enthusiasm. Your goal at the interview is to generate a job offer, so you should find it easy to avoid the crimes that damage your case:

Don'ts:

1. Do not discuss salary, vacation, or benefits. It is not that the questions are invalid, just that the timing is wrong. Bringing these topics up before you have an offer is asking what the company can do for you; instead, you should be saying what you can do for the company. These topics are part of the negotiation, and without an offer you have nothing to negotiate.

2. Don't press for an early decision. Interviewees

should ask: "When will I know your decision?" On hearing the answer, however, they should *not* ask for a decision to be made earlier. And *don't* try to use "the-other-opportunities-I-have-to-consider" gambit as leverage. This annoys the interviewer, makes you look foolish, and makes you negotiate from a position of weakness. Timing is everything, and how to handle "other opportunities" as leverage, *correctly*, is handled later in section IV.

3. Don't show discouragement. Sometimes a job offer can occur on the spot. Most times it does not. Don't show discouragement if you are not offered the job at the interview, because it shows a lack of self-esteem and determination. Avoiding a bad impression is merely the foundation of leaving a good one. The right image to leave is one of enthusiasm, guts, and openness—just the traits you have been projecting throughout the interview.

4. Don't ask for an evaluation of your interview performance. That forces the issue and puts the interviewer in an awkward position.

Dos:

1. When the opportunity comes to ask any final questions, review your notes. Bring up any relevant strengths that haven't been addressed. Ask job-related questions.

2. Show decisiveness. If you are offered the job, accept it with enthusiasm. Lock it up now and put yourself in control; you can always change your mind later.

3. When you are interviewed by more than one person, be sure you have the correct spelling of their names. "I enjoyed meeting your colleagues, Ms. Smith. Could you give me the correct spelling of their names, please?" This question will give you the names you forgot in the heat of battle, and will demonstrate your consideration.

4. Review the job's requirements with the inter-

viewer and match them point by point with your skills and attributes.

5. *Find out if this is the only interview.* If so, you must ask for the job in a positive and enthusiastic manner. Find out the time-frame for a decision and finish with: "I am very enthusiastic about the job and the contributions I can make. If your decision will be made by the 15th, what must I do in the meantime to assure I get the job?"

6. *Ask for the next interview.* When there are subsequent interviews in the hiring procedure, ask for the next interview in the same honest and forthright manner. "Is now a good time to schedule our next meeting?" If you do not ask, you do not get.

7. *A good leading question to ask is, "Until I hear from you again, what particular aspects of the job and this interview should I be considering?"*

8. *Always depart in the same polite and assured manner with which you entered.* Look the interviewer in the eyes, put a smile in your baby blues (there's no need to grin), give a firm handshake, and say, "This has been an exciting meeting for me. This is a job I can do, and I feel I can contribute to your goals, because the atmosphere here seems conducive to doing my very best work. When will we speak again?"

IV

Finishing Touches

The successful completion of the first meeting is a big stride toward getting job offers, yet it is not the end of your job hunt.

A company rarely hires the first competent person it sees. In the climate of the 80s, a company has a vast field from which to choose. A hiring manager will sometimes interview as many as 15 people for a particular job, but the strain and pace of conducting interviews naturally dim the memory of each applicant. Unless you are the last person to be interviewed, the impression you make will fade with each subsequent interview the interviewer undertakes. And if you are not remembered, you will not be offered the job. You must develop a strategy to keep your name and skills constantly in the forefront of the interviewer's mind. These finishing touches often make all the difference.

Some of the suggestions here may not seem earth-shattering, but merely a demonstration of your manners, enthusiasm, and determination. But remember that today *all* employers are looking for people with that extra little *something,* so you must avoid the negative (or indifferent) impression that is created when you ignore these guidelines.

19.
Out of Sight,
Out of Mind

The first thing you do on leaving the interview is breathe a sigh of relief. The second is to make sure that "out of sight, out of mind" will not apply to you. You do this by starting a follow-up procedure immediately after the interview.

Sitting in your car, on the bus, train, or plane, do a written recap of the interview while it's still fresh in your mind. Answer these questions:

- Whom did you meet? Names and titles.

- What does the job entail?

- Why can you do the job?

- What aspects of the interview went poorly? Why?

- What is the agreed-upon next step?

- What was said during the last few minutes of the interview?

Probably the most difficult—and most important—thing to do is to analyze what aspects of the interview went poorly. A person does not get offered a job based solely on strength. On the contrary, many people get new jobs based on their relative lack of negatives as compared to the other applicants. So, it is *mandatory* that you look for and recognize any negatives from your performance. This is the only way you will have an opportunity to package and overcome those negatives in your follow-up procedure and during subsequent interviews.

The next step is to write the follow-up letter to the interviewer to acknowledge the meeting, and keep you fresh in his or her mind.

1. Type the letter. It exhibits greater professionalism. If you don't own a typewriter, the local library will frequently allow the use of theirs. If not, a typing service will do it for a nominal fee. If, for any reason, the letter cannot be typed, make sure it is legibly and neatly written. The letter should make three points clear to the company representative:

- You paid attention to what was being said

- You understood the importance of the inter-viewer's comments

- You are excited about the job, can do it, and want it

2. Use the right words and phrases in your letter. Here are some you might want to use:

- *Upon reflection,* and, *Having thought about our meeting* . . .

- *Recognize*—"I recognize the importance of..."

- *Listen*—"Listening to the points you made..."

- *Enthusiasm, enthusiastic*—Let the interviewer catch your enthusiasm. It is very effective, especially as your letter will arrive while other applicants are nervously sweating their way through the interview.

- *Impressed*—Let the interviewer know you were impressed with the people/product/service/facility/market/position, but *do not overkill.*

- *Challenge*—Feel you would be challenged to do your best work in this environment.

- *Confidence*—There is a job to be done and a challenge to be met. Let the interviewer know you are confident of doing both well.

- *Interest*—If you want the job/next interview, say so. At this stage, the company is buying and you are selling. Ask for the job in a positive and enthusiastic manner.

- *Appreciation*—As a courtesy and mark of professional manners, you must express appreciation for the time the interviewer took out of his or her busy schedule.

3. Whenever possible and appropriate, mention the names of the people you met at the interview. Draw attention to one of the topics that was of general interest to the interviewer(s).

4. Your follow-up letter will be addressed to the main interviewer. Send a copy to personnel with a note of thanks as a courtesy.

5. Mail the letter within 24 hours of the interview. If the decision is going to be made in the next couple of days, hand-deliver the letter or make a strong point by sending a mailgram. The follow-up letter will help to set you apart from other applicants and will refresh your image in the mind of the interviewer just when it would normally be starting to dim.

6. If you do not hear anything after five days, which is quite normal, put in a telephone call to the company representative. Reiterate the points made in the letter, saying that you want the job/next interview, and finish your statements with a question: "Mr. Smith, I feel confident about my ability to contribute to your department's efforts and I really want the job. Could you tell me what I have to do to get it?" Then be quiet and wait for the answer.

□ □ □

Of course, you may be told you are no longer in the running. The next chapter will show you that this is a *great* opportunity to snatch victory from the jaws of defeat.

20.
Snatching Victory from the Jaws of Defeat

During the interviewing process, there are bound to be interviewers who *erroneously* come to the conclusion that you are not the right person for the job they need to fill. When this happens, you will be turned down. This absurd travesty of justice can occur in different ways:

- At the interview

- In a letter of rejection

- During your follow-up telephone call

Whenever the turn-down comes, you must be emotionally and intellectually prepared to take advantage of the *opportunity* being offered to you.

When you get turned down for the only opportunity you have going, the rejection can be devastating to your ego. That is why I have stressed throughout the wisdom of having at least a few interviews in process at the same time. This naturally does not apply if you are fortunate enough to be represented by a skilled personnel consultant. He or she will naturally have lined you up with the best opportunities to begin with.

You *will* get turned down. No one can be right for every job. However, the right person for a job doesn't always get it; the best prepared and most determined often does. While you in part may be responsible for the initial rejection, you still have the power to correct the situation and win the job offer. What you do with the claimed victory is a different matter; you will then be in a seller's market with choice and control of your situation.

To correct this requires only willpower and determination. Almost every job you desire is obtainable once you understand the hiring process from the interviewer's side of the desk. Your initial—and temporary—rejection is attributable to only one of these reasons:

- Interviewer does not feel you can do the job

- Interviewer feels you lack a successful profile

- Interviewer did not feel your personality would contribute to the smooth functioning of the department

With belief in yourself, you can still succeed. Repeat to yourself constantly through the interview cycle: "I will get this job, no one else can give as much to this company as I can!" Do this and implement the following plan immediately when you hear of rejection, whether in person, via mail, or over the telephone.

☐ *Step One:* Thank the interviewer for the time and consideration. Then ask politely: "To help my future job search, why wasn't I chosen for the position?" Assure the interviewer that you would truly appreciate honest and objective reasoning. Listen to the reply and do not interrupt regardless of the comments. Use your time constructively and take notes furiously. When the company representative finishes speaking, show you understood the comments. (Remember, understanding and agreeing are different animals.)

"Thank you, Mr. Smith, now I can understand the way you feel. Because I am not a professional interviewer, I'm afraid my interview nerves got in the way. I'm very interested in working for your company *[use an enthusiastic tone]*, and am determined to get the job. Let me meet with you once again. This time, when I'm not so nervous, I am confident you will see I really do have the skills/attributes you require *[then provide an example of a skill you have in the questionable area]*. You name the time and the place, and I will be there. What's best for you, Mr. Smith?''

End with a question, of course. An enthusiastic request like this is very difficult to refuse and will usually get you another interview. An interview, of course, at which you *must* shine.

□ *Step Two:* Check your notes and accept the company representative's concerns. Their validity is irrelevant; the important point is that these negative points represent the problem areas in the interviewer's perception of you. List the negative perceptions, and using the techniques, exercises, and Value Keys discussed throughout the book, develop different ways to overcome or compensate for every negative perception.

□ *Step Three:* Re-read section III.

□ *Step Four:* Practice aloud the statements and responses you will use at the interview. If you can practice with someone who plays the part of the interviewer, so much the better. This will create a real interview atmosphere and be helpful to your success.

□ *Step Five:* Study *all* available information on the company.

□ *Step Six:* Congratulate yourself continually for getting another interview after initial rejection. This is proof of your self-worth, ability, and tenacity. You have nothing to lose and everything to gain, having already risen phoenix-like from the ashes of temporary defeat.

□ *Step Seven:* During the interview, ask for the job in a positive and enthusiastic manner. Your drive and staying power will impress the interviewer. All you must do to win the job is overcome the perceived negatives, and you have been given the time to prepare. Go for it.

□ *Step Eight:* Even when all has failed at the subsequent interview, do not leave without a final request for the job. Play your trump card: "Mr. Smith, I respect the fact that you allowed me the opportunity to prove myself here today. I am convinced I am the best person for the job. I want you to give me a trial and I will prove on the job that I am the best hiring decision you have made this year. Will you give us both the opportunity?''

Most people fail in their endeavors by quitting just before the dawn of success. Follow these directions and you can win the job. You have proved yourself to be a fighter and that is universally admired. The company representative will want you to succeed because you are made of stuff that is rarely seen today. You are a person of guts, drive, and endurance, the hallmarks of a winner. Job turn-downs are an opportunity to exercise and build your strengths, and you may well add to your growing number of job offers.

21.
Multiple Interviews, Multiple Offers

False optimism and laziness lead many job hunters to be content with only one interview in process at any given time. This severely reduces the odds of landing the best job in town within your chosen time-frame. It further guarantees that you will continue to operate in a buyer's market.

The recommended approach is to generate as many interviews as possible in a two- to three-week period. Interviewing skills are learned, and necessarily improve with practice. With the improved skills comes a greater confidence, and those natural interview nerves disperse. Your confidence shows through to potential employers, and you are perceived in a positive light. And because other companies are interested in you, everyone will move more quickly to secure your services. This is especially important if you are unfortunate enough to be unemployed. Being out of work is when you need money the most and is the time when the salary you can command on the open market is substantially reduced. The interview activity you generate will help offset this.

By generating multiple interviews, you bring the time of the first job offer closer and closer. That one job offer can be quickly parlayed into a number of others. And with a single job offer, your unemployed status has, to all intents and purposes, passed.

Immediately you can call every company with whom you've met, and explain the situation. "Mr. Johnson, I'm calling because while still under consideration with your company I have received a job offer from one of your competitors. I would hate to make a decision without the chance of speaking with you again. I was very impressed by my meeting with you. Can we get together in the next couple of days?" End, of course, with a question that carries the conversation forward.

If you were in the running at all, your call will usually generate another interview; Mr. Johnson does not want to miss out on a suddenly prized commodity. Remember: it is human nature to want the very things one is about to lose. So you see, your simple offer can be multiplied almost by the number of interviews you have in process at the time.

A single job offer can also be used to generate interviews with new firms. It is as simple as making your usual telephone networking presentation, but ending it differently. You would be very interested in meeting with them because of (your knowledge of the company/ product/service). But also because you have just received a job offer: Would it be possible to get together in the next couple of days?

Relying on one interview at a time can only lead to prolonged anxiety, disappointment, and possibly unemployment. This reliance is due to the combination of false optimism, laziness, and fear of rejection. These are traits that cannot be tolerated except by confirmed defeatists, for defeat is the inevitable result of these traits. As Heraclitus said, "Character is destiny." In the employment business we say, "The job offer that cannot fail will."

Self-esteem, on the other hand, is vital to your success, and happiness is found with it. And with it you will begin to awake each day with a vitality previously unknown. Vigor will increase, your enthusiasm will rise, and desire to achieve will burn within. The more you do today, the better you will feel tomorrow.

Even when you follow this plan to the letter, not every interview will result in an offer. But with many irons in the fire, an occasional firm rejection should not affect your morale. If it does, grow up! This won't be the first or last time you face rejection. Be persistent, and above all, close your mind to all negative and discouraging influences. The success you experience from implementing this plan will increase your store of willpower and determination, penetrate to the core of your being, effect the successful outcome of your job hunt, and enrich your whole life. Start today. The key to your success is preparation. Remember, it is necessary to plan and organize in order to get rich. Staying poor is easy; poverty needs no effort. Tomorrow never comes, so start building that well-stocked briefcase today.

Conclusion:
The Glittering Prizes

It's time for action, to wrestle job offers from the other contenders at the job interview. All victories have their foundation in careful
preparation, and in finishing *Knock 'em Dead,* you are loaded for bear
and ready for the hunt.

Your winning attitude is positive and active (dream jobs don't come to
those who sit and wait), you realize success depends on getting out and
generating interviews for yourself. At these interviews you will main-
tain the interviewer's interest and attention by carrying your half of the
conversation. What you ask will show your interest, demonstrate your
analytical abilities, and carry the conversation forward.   If in doubt
about the meaning of a question, you will ask one of your own to clarify
it

The corporate body recognizes its most valuable resources in those
employees who understand and contribute towards its goals.   These
people have something in common: they all recognize their differing
jobs as a series of challenges and problems; each to be anticipated, met,
and solved. It's this attitude that lands jobs and helps careers.

People like this advance their careers faster than others, because
they possess a critical awareness of universally-admired business

practices and value systems. They then leverage their careers by projecting the personality traits that most closely complement those practices and values.

As I said at the beginning of this book, a job interview is a ritualized mating dance. The name of that dance is "attitude." Now that you know the steps, you are ready to whirl away with the glittering prizes. There is no more to say except: go to your next interview and *knock 'em dead.*

Bibliography

Some of the books listed here can be bought inexpensively at a bookstore. Most, however, are expensive, so you will find it cost-effective to go to your local library to use them. Many states have an inter-library lending system, so if the book you want is not available, the librarian can usually get it for you.

As mentioned earlier, do not rely *solely* on reference books. Their size and scope often makes them a little out of date, and they aren't all updated or published every year. Ask your librarian for the most recent editions.

General Guides and Directories:

Billion Dollar Directory: America's Corporate Families. Dun & Bradstreet: New York, NY.

Lists companies alphabetically, geographically, and by product, and charts the various divisions and subdivisions of major corporations.

Dun's Employment Opportunities Directory/The Career Guide. Dun & Bradstreet: New York, NY.

A guide to over 4000 companies, including identifying information, (names, titles, addresses, and phone numbers); a brief history of the company and its line of business; an overview of career opportunities; and the educational specialties the company hires.

The National Job Bank. Bob Adams, Inc.: Boston, MA.

A comprehensive directory that lists more than 8000 major employers

(300 or more employees) alphabetically for each state and the District of Columbia. Contains contact information, a description of the business, common positions filled, educational backgrounds sought, and fringe benefits offered. Also provides industrial/geographical cross-index.

Standard & Poor's Register of Corporations, Directors, and Executives. Standard & Poor's (McGraw-Hill): New York, NY.

Comes in three volumes. The first lists all major companies by industry and geography; the second gives the details and contact information on those companies; the third gives personal data on many corporate executives.

State Manufacturing Directories.

Every state has one. It uses a form similar to the *Standard & Poor's Register.* It usually comes in one volume, has contact data for the various companies, but has no personal information about executives. Repeats some information from the *Standard & Poor's Register,* but also includes many smaller, local companies.

Thomas Register of American Manufacturers. Thomas Publishing Company: New York.

A enormous (12-volume) manufacturing business-to-business directory. Thousands of large and small companies in every field.

Other Guides:

[Content information for the following directories, and thousands of other reference sources, can be found in: *Directory of Directories:* Gale Research Company: Detroit, MI. Every good library should have one.]

Access. National Association of Personnel Consultants: Washington, DC.

Bay Area Employer Directory. James Albin: Sausalito, CA.

Bay Area Employment Agency and Executive Recruiter Directory. James Albin: Sausalito, CA.

Boston Job Bank. Bob Adams, Inc.: Boston, MA.

Career Employment Opportunities Directory. Ready Reference Press: Santa Monica, CA.

Career Guide to Professional Associations: A Directory of Organizations by Occupational Field. Carroll Press: Cranston, RI.

Career Opportunities Index. Career Research Systems: Huntington Beach, CA.

College Placement Annual. College Placement Council: Bethlehem, PA.

Directory of Career Planning and Placement Offices. College Placement Council: Bethlehem, PA.

Directory of Summer Jobs Abroad. Vacation-Work: Oxford, England.

Executive Employment Guide. Management Information Service: New York, NY.

Federal Career Opportunities. Federal Research Service Inc.: Vienna, VA.

Federal Job Information Centers Directory. Office of Personnel Management: Washington, DC.

Federal Jobs. U.S. Government Printing Office: Leesburg, VA.

Greater Atlanta Job Bank. Bob Adams, Inc.: Boston, MA.

Greater Chicago Job Bank. Bob Adams, Inc.: Boston, MA.

International Jobs: Where They Are, How to Get Them. Addison-Wesley Publishing Company: Reading, MA.

Job Catalog. Mail Order USA: Washington, DC.

Job Hunter's Guide to 8 Great American Cities. Brattle Publications: Cambridge, MA.

Job Hunter's Guide to the Rocky Mountain West. Brattle Publications: Cambridge, MA.

Job Hunter's Guide to Seattle. Alex Collections: Seattle, WA.

Job Hunter's Guide to the Sunbelt. Brattle Publications: Cambridge, MA.

Metropolitan New York Job Bank. Bob Adams, Inc.: Boston, MA.

Metropolitan Washington (DC) Job Bank. Bob Adams, Inc.: Boston, MA.

Multinational Marketing and Employment Directory. World Trade Academy Press: New York, NY.

Northwest Job Bank. Bob Adams, Inc.: Boston, MA.

Ohio Job Bank. Bob Adams, Inc.: Boston, MA.

Pennsylvania Job Bank. Bob Adams, Inc.: Boston, MA.

Seasonal Employment. National Park Service, Department of the Interior: Washington, DC.

San Francisco/Bay Area Job Bank. Bob Adams, Inc.: Boston, MA.

Southern California Job Bank. Bob Adams, Inc.: Boston, MA.

Southwest Job Bank. Bob Adams, Inc.: Boston, MA.

Summer Employment Directory of the United States. Writers Digest Books: Cincinnati, OH.

Summer Jobs: Opportunities in Federal Government. Office of Personnel Management: Washington, DC.

Texas Job Bank. Bob Adams, Inc.: Boston, MA.

Transactions, Resource Guide to Work, Travel and Study Abroad. Clayton A. Hubbs: Amherst, MA.

Whole World Handbook. Council of International Educational Exchange: New York, NY.

Especially for Women:

AWIS Job Bulletin. Association for Women in Science: Washington, DC.

Blue Collar Jobs for Women. E.P. Dutton Inc.: New York, NY.

Catalyst National Network of Career Resource Centers. Catalyst: New York, NY.

Directory of Career Resources for Women. Ready Reference Press: Santa Monica, CA.

Displaced Homemaker Program Directory. Displaced Homemakers Network: Washington, DC.

Internship Programs for Women. National Society for Internships: Washington, DC.

National Directory of Women's Employment Programs: Who They Are, What They Do. Wider Opportunities for Women: Washington, DC.

Professional Women's Groups. American Association of University Women: Washington, DC.

Resource Directory for Affirmative Recruitment in Connecticut. Connecticut Commission of Human Rights: Hartford, CT.

Women Helping Women: A State by State Directory of Services. Women's Action Alliance: New York, NY.

Women's Guide to Career Preparation. Anchor Press (Doubleday): New York, NY.

Women's Guide to Apprenticeship. Women's Bureau, U.S. Department of Labor: Washington, DC.

Especially for Minorities:

Career Development Opportunities for Native Americans. Office of Indian Educational Programs, Bureau of Indian Affairs, Department of the Interior: Washington, DC.

Directory of Career Resources for Minorities. Ready Reference Press: Santa Monica, CA.

Directory of Special Programs for Minority Group Members: Career Information Services, Employment Skills Banks, Financial Aid Services. Garrett Park Press: Garrett Park, MD.

Index to
the Questions

What difficulties do you have tolerating people with different backgrounds and interests from yours? **115**

What do you feel is a satisfactory attendance record? **103**

What do you know about our company? **142**

What do you think determines progress in a good company? **151**

What do you think of your current/last boss? **110**

What have you done that shows initiative and willingness to work? **111, 149**

What have you learned from the jobs you have held? **93**

What have your other jobs taught you? **114**

What interests you least about this job? **102**

What interests you most about this job? **91**

What is an adequate reward for your efforts? **154**

What is the least relevant job you have held? **156**

What is the most difficult situation you have faced? **147**

What is the worst thing you have heard about our company? **133**

What is your energy level like? Describe a particular day. **85**

What is your general impression of your last company? **103**

What is your greatest strength? **90**

What is your greatest weakness? **99**

What kind of decisions are most difficult for you? **100**

What kind of experience do you have for this job? **86**

What kind of people do you find it difficult to work with? **105**

What kind of things do you worry about? **155**

What personal characteristics are necessary for success in your field? **113**

What qualifications do you have that will make you successful in this field? **150**

What type of decisions did you make on your last job? **94**